THE PENGUIN'S PROGRESS

Eric Merry

ISBN-10:1-946560-02-2

ISBN-13: 978-1-946560-02-5

Edited by The Editing Hall

Formatting by Anessa Books

Published by Plato Publishing

CHAPTER ONE

FOR KING & COUNTRY

DURING THE WARM SUNNY DAYS of early September 1940, I used to cycle into Kent from London to watch the air war I so desperately wanted to join. For me in those early weeks, the war consisted of trails in the sky, machine gun noises high in the heavens, planes zooming about, and whistling bombs. The steady pattern of the bombers coming over was broken up by the British fighters, which dropped through the German formations like stones. The odd bomber fluttered to earth like a leaf caught in the wind.

Others were hurled down like flaming arrows, leaving a funeral pall of smoke where they met the yellow corn and green grass, scarring the countryside with their machines as well as with their bombs.

On one occasion, I recall seeing several fighters sweep through a valley at zero feet. From my grassy slope, I watched an attack on the RAF fighter station at Biggin Hill. Later a Dornier bomber came through, spewing oily smoke from an engine, closely pursued by a Spitfire. I felt pride in those who became "the few," as I absorbed the sights, the sounds, the smells, the roar of aircraft engines, the rat-a-tat of machine guns, the thrills of seeing the enemy going down. Now, it is hard to justify the tremendous enthusiasm it all generated in me.

On 12 September 1940, I became 18 years old. Knowing everything the world had to offer, I made my decision within days of my birthday. I volunteered for the RAF at the Air Ministry in Kingsway, London. I was allocated an appointment time for the first of many of the selection boards I would have to negotiate before being accepted. They were very fussy in the early days, and there was a selection panel to decide if you were suitable material to even take a medical.

Passing the medical allowed you to go before another panel, which would decide if you could go forward to the Air Vocation Board, which assessed you for a specific air training. At last, I was given a date and time to be at Euston House in London, a huge medical complex. My mother, Aggie, was distraught at the idea of her only son being "up there" and consoled herself with the thought I might fail the medical and be sent home.

My father, Edward Thomas Merry, was a Royal Marine. At the time of my enlistment, he was away helping to setting up the special R.M. Services that later became the Commandos. He had joined as a regular in 1916 and was discharged in December 1937 at 38 years of age as a pensioner. He was recalled in September 1938 at the time of the Munich crisis.

I had returned to Deal with him. He did not come out of the service again until the end of the war, ending his career in India as Quartermaster General of the Royal Marines in Asia. I had been a "cadet" from the age of nine. At  sixteen, I became a "boy marine" with the view of a Royal Marine career. It was to be the bitterest pill for my father when I did not follow him into the Marines.

However, on the appointed day and time, I presented myself at Euston House and was immediately handed a not-too-large towel and told to strip. For the whole of that day and the next, dozens of hopeful young lads and I ran from one room to another, submitting to this test here and that test there. I remember a medical orderly telling me my "sugars were out of balance" and advised me to drink quarts of water to "flush it through." I drank and drank until I nearly burst, it was so important to me.

At the end of two days, I was adjudged A.1. fit for aircrew duties. I crawled back home to Camberwell with the grand-daddy of all colds. I said to my mother, "If I hadn't been told how fit I was, I would be sure that I was dying." Before I left Euston House, I was given orders to be at the Kingsway Air Ministry at the crack of dawn on 11 November 1940.

At Kingsway, I appeared before another Board that would finally decide how I was best suited to help win the war! The Air Vocation Board consisted of a terrifying group of senior air force officers arrayed behind a great long table. I recall the impression that my lack of academic achievements, and the fact that they had never heard of the Royal Marine School of which I was so proud, proved to be a drawback. I was not, therefore, considered pilot material. They did, however, offer me the chance of flying in the capacity of Wireless Operator/Air Gunner, which I readily accepted.

After waiting around for what seemed ages, I was ushered into a room laid out like a classroom with about two dozen other young hopefuls. There were bibles on the desks, and an officer asked us to pick them up and repeat an oath. We were being sworn in when he stopped abruptly and asked us to stand to attention "for the dead of the last war" (1914-1918). The whole of The Great War seemed to go through my mind as I stood there: pictures of the trenches, mud, mutilation, death, WW1 tanks, aeroplanes, airships, and graves. Then a voice returned me to the present.

"Gentlemen."

At exactly two minutes past eleven on the 11 November 1940, I swore to serve my King and Country. As the officer remarked, we would always remember that precise moment, and I have! As I left, I was given a piece of paper with my name and number on it. The number was 1381917. From another room, I was given a leave pass, a ten-shilling note, and a rail ticket to Cardington.

My mother cried when I told her I was officially in the air force. She had secretly hoped they would not take me and had not mentioned it to my father in her letters. Quite by chance, he came home for the weekend.

When I said I had signed on, he laughingly asked me, "What took you so long?" From the tone in his voice, I have always suspected he knew something was amiss.

I was 18 years and two months old. When I told him I had to report to Cardington (not to Chatham, Portsmouth or Plymouth—Royal Marine depots) the realisation that I had actually joined the RAF and not the Marines hit him like a sledge hammer. He turned away and hardly spoke a word to my mother or me before he went back to his war. Timothy, a pet name for Dad but Tom to most people, went to Havant in Hampshire before going north to the Isle of Arran for the development of the Commando concept and the Green Beret. I went to Cardington and thence to Morecambe for "square bashing"—learning how to march and drill. That was to be followed by Gunnery School and some preliminary wireless training at Calshot near Southampton.

It was at Calshot that I met Cyril Morgan. Through him, I met his sister Berenice, who became my life partner after the war.

WHEN "TIMOTHY" AND I left to go to war, Aggie had given her all. Her husband had returned to the Royal Marines and her only son to the air force. Then she did a really brave thing but typical of her. She packed up our home and returned to her native town of Harwich. With the support of friends and family, she began the hopeful process of preparing a place for her men to come back to. She didn't know that it would be nearly five years before we were to meet as a family again. Or if we would ever return again for that matter!

So off to Cardington in Bedfordshire to become an airman!

CHAPTER TWO

CIVILIAN to SERVICEMAN

AN ASSORTED GROUP OF CIVILIANS assembled on the windy parade ground of the RAF depot at Cardington in Bedfordshire. We were to begin the transformation from private citizens into a crew of uniformed airmen. We started the conversion by going through the old R.101 airship hangar to collect our ill-fitting uniforms, big boots, as well as all the other paraphernalia of a serviceman. Our civilian clothes were then parcelled up and sent home without a covering letter. Heaven alone knows what effect that had on my mother!

Cardington was my first introduction to the army hut, although the battleship grey linoleum of a barrack room was no stranger to me. Lino so deeply polished that it looked as though the whole floor was a sheet of glass and squeaked as one walked gingerly across it. The coal scuttles with their shiny, dusted, and correctly sized pieces of coal that no one ever burned. The tall cast-iron ebony black round stoves on their white washed surrounds stood like proud sentries at each end of the hut.

Drawn up outside the huts, the forty new inmates of the squad listened to the corporal's first list of "do's and don'ts." Behind my back, I idly slipped my china mug from one finger to another. Just as the corporal said, "Any airman breaking his mug will have to reimburse the Air Council with six pence," mine went crashing to the ground! Some of the blokes thought it funny, but I just felt a bit of an idiot. They introduced metal mugs later, so perhaps I wasn't the only fool to join the air force. We then had a group picture taken outside the hut, and I proudly sent it home.

Cardington was the initial shoe-horning of civilians into the service life, but it was still all very civilized at this stage. The corporal said, "I'll call your name and last three (of ones service number) and you'll answer with 'Sir'. Got it?"

Indeed, I should have "got it" because of my long but youthful marine tradition and my familiarity with service numbers. However, this RAF number was one million, three hundred eighty-one thousand, nine hundred and seventeen, 1381917. I had it written on a piece of paper and kept saying to myself, "My last three are nine hundred and seventeen— nine seventeen."

I came to at the corporal's exasperated voice, "Come on nine-one-seven Merry, I know you're here." Oh my God! I realised it was me.

"Sir?"

"Thank you, Mister Merry." I can still remember how stupid I felt.

The forty of us were allocated a hut, and

I was elected Head Man because I was the youngest. Seemed logical at the time. Some of them were as old as 25! It took a few hectic days to get used to the very early mornings, especially the cold washes and shaves (it was November of 1940), the awful smell of the cookhouse, and the crowded mess hall. We were quickly organised, equipped, and bundled up by train to Morecambe in Lancashire within a few days.

As we marched from the railway station through the town, we were counted off into seaside guesthouses like refugees, but we were ready and keen for our new experience. The drill squad! This was where we would learn how to march, and counter-march; this was where we would learn how to handle a rifle, salute and become proper service men. This is where I shone because of my life-long association with the Royal Marines, a fact not lost on our drill corporal who used to lean against the seawall while I "took the squad."

For the next 30 days, we slowly became a competent unit of men wheeling and drilling, as real soldiers do, in the face of the chilly winds that came in from Morecambe Bay. We spent many hours stomping up and down the frozen sea front, past the boarded up entertainment booths and the parade of shops. In the summer time of previous years, this beach would have had throngs of gay and happy people with candy floss. The billet landlady looked after us like paying guests, because that's what we were to her, and out of season visitors at that!

In due time, we passed out on a great parade, and later, we received our individual postings to various parts of the country. The square-bashing squads had been made up of airmen of all trades. Now was the time for each man or group to go to the various trade and flying schools or on to the holding stations, prior to their specific training.

CHAPTER THREE

THE PENGUIN FLIES

I WAS POSTED WAY DOWN south to Calshot in Hampshire, a flying boat station about 20 miles south of Southampton on the Solent. I was so very pleased at the prospect of being on a Coastal Command Air Station.

The living quarters and main camp were about two miles from the actual air station, with its huge hangers built on the end of the long spit of land jutting out into the Solent. The land spit is curled somewhat like a bent finger, trapping a flat marshy area in its crook. When I arrived at the Calshot guard house, I was booked in and given a hut. As I entered, I was greeted by an "old hand" (he had arrived the day before) who welcomed me warmly. It was Cyril Morgan, and for as long as we were able, we were firm friends.

SUNDERLAND
Four Engine Reconnaissance Flying Boat
Wing Span 113 ft. Length 85 ft. Height (Top of fin) 33 ft.
Armament Eight o.303" in three power operated turrets
(Two in front, two amidships and four in tail unit plus two beam guns).
Bombs and depth charges wound out on racks under wing
Crew Two pilots, radio operator, navigator, engineer, 3 power operated gunners, bomb aimer/cook, plus two beam gunners

I couldn't get down to the hangers fast enough, and Cyril was game to come down with me to see the flying boats that were there. The Sunderlands were extremely large and carried eight, sometimes ten in crew. They patrolled the English Channel and the Western Approaches to meet convoys and into the Bay of Biscay to catch U-boats close to their bases. The other aeroplane used was the old fashioned Saro London flying boat (sometimes called the Walrus). It had great wide upper wings and an engine suspended high in the rigging above a fuselage that made it look more like a motorboat than an aeroplane. An open gun cockpit in the front of the fuselage had a surrounding circular metal bar called a scarf ring, on which was mounted either a Lewis or Vickers machine gun. This gun position was situated on the tip of the hull and was reached by crawling on one's hands and knees through the claustrophobic bottom of the hull. I was to learn my gunnery skills in these aircraft that owed more to World War 1 than to World War 2.

The normal camp routine took over, and once again (I was to think it often until I matured a little) I thought the war would be over before I could get into it. The C.O. was very aircrew minded and insisted that we wore the  distinctive aircrew under training "white flash" in our caps. (It was here that I adopted the personal mascot of a penguin, a flightless sea bird with white underparts. I little realised that I would spend the majority of the war not flying.) We were rather proud of our white flash, even though it was a boastful thing. Nevertheless, it did carry certain privileges on the camp because we were excused many tiresome chores like guard duties. We spent many hours in practical and theoretical gunnery, and I particularly remember Cyril and I practising stripping the guns down with fingers bound together (duplicating frozen hands) and blindfolded (just in case we couldn't see). Cyril was not too good at this. His gunnery left much to be desired and he could never make a good deflection shot, but he came into his own with Morse code. However, although I was good at gunnery I was always struggling with the Morse code.

I spent a great deal of my free time in the Calshot library and discovered that a very special airman had been there before me, "Lawrence of Arabia." Lawrence fostered a rebellion of Arabs against the Turks during WWI, thereby helping Britain because the Turks were allies of Germany. Lawrence wrote a book called *The Seven Pillars of Wisdom*, which was hailed by Winston Churchill as one of the greatest books ever written in the English language as a narrative of war and adventure. But as famous as he was, Lawrence joined the RAF between the wars as an ordinary airman under the name of Shaw, and as Shaw, he looked after the Calshot library. I was fascinated with the thoughts of Shaw and spent the majority of my spare time in the library where I found many interesting notes, pictures, and other mementos of his stay there. He was killed riding his motorbike excessively fast in a Dorset country lane.

WALRUS
Single Engine Amphibian Flying Boat
Wing span 46 . Length 37 ft
Armament. Bow cockpit gunner with Scarff ring (Vickers or Lewis gun). Aft gunner with special mounting
Crew Pilot, navigator/wireless operator, one or two air gunners.

The routine of gunnery training (and Morse practise) went on apace, and I was soon very proficient at one if not the other. I always consoled myself with the thought that the wireless school was still to come, so I threw myself wholeheartedly into the art of air gunnery. In due time, I passed my gunnery with a very high score while failing miserably with my pre-school

Morse and wireless capabilities.

But back to gunnery, crouched and cramped in the Walrus cabin, I would tingle as the "old gal," vibrating through her whole being,  taxied out on the choppy water. As the engine roared, the water smashing against the hull sounded like a hundred boys hitting corrugated iron with sticks. Then the water noise ceased as the aircraft gently lifted, and the engine note changed (while the draughts inside the plane increased!). A nod from the skipper and the crawl on one's hands and knees began through what we called the "scuppers," our head coming up into the howling freezing gale. It was a struggle to clip the heavy gun onto the scarf ring. It was also difficult to get the ammunition pans from the racks on to the firing position of the gun with frozen fingers. But you did, and once you settled down, you gave the first tentative look around the hostile sky.

THE WALRUS WAS designated by the Royal Navy as an observer plane. In the early days, the Coastal Command used it to rescue downed aircrew in the English Channel. It was also used as a training platform for rookie air gunners from its front open cockpit. However, because of its lack of speed and defensive armament it was eventually withdrawn from the Channel rescue operations. Walruses were frequently shot down by German fighters operating from the French coast. The losses became intolerable so the rescue missions were aborted and it was left to power boats to collect the pilots etc. who found themselves in the Channel swell. The only time I was scheduled for this harrowing duty, we were flagged to return as we were taxing out from the jetty. The order to rescind those 'ops' had just come in.

BY THE TIME I had passed as an L.A.C. Air Gunner, new things were happening in the air force. Pan loading guns were obsolescent, and extremely fast firing Browning guns were coming in freely on bombers and being fitted into power-operated turrets.

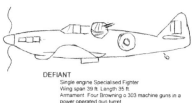

DEFIANT
Single engine Specialised Fighter
Wing span 39 ft. Length 35 ft.
Armament: Four Browning o 303 machine guns in a
power operated gun turret
Crew: Pilot. Power operated Air Gunner

They were already on Sunderlands' front and rear turrets and the new Boulton Paul Defiant fighter plane was designed around this power-operated gun turret. In fact, the C.O. had a special gun turret installed on the top of the water tower, and he 'allowed' his favourite "white flash" airmen to assist the RAF Regiment and Army A.A. teams to defend the station from enemy attacks, which were spasmodic but briefly intense.

I have always believed that I brought a Messerschmitt 109 down. Although everyone was having a go at it as it swept across the Spit from the Solent, it actually came within 100 yards of the tower, ran across the steady stream of the four Browning guns I was firing, and ended up on the mud flats. The pilot was killed and an inspection of the plane showed it peppered along its whole length. The

C.O. quietly credited the "tower" with it, but Cyril and the lads were not so quiet about it, as you may imagine. It seems terrible now to remember how elated I felt!

I had a number of long range patrols in Sunderlands from Calshot. These planes had some of the earliest 0.5 inch free swinging machine guns fitted in the midship areas. The ammunition was belt fed into a square port hole. The gunners were stabilized by a strap around the waist, secured to the fuselage. I crewed as the port side midship's gunner.

As a young marine, I always had difficulty in remembering which side was Port or Starboard and the colour that goes with them. Timothy gave me an aide-mémoire, "Port (wine) is red and is always left except on the table." The Sunderland was constantly being modified with extra guns etc., to such an extent that the Germans apparently nicknamed it The Porcupine. It seemed natural for me to choose the port side as my gun spot, as my compatriot didn't seem to care anyway. I was to have no idea of the consequences of that decision.

They were usually uneventful missions, other than the excitement generated by  the long air journeys over the Atlantic to meet ships way out there somewhere. A convoy of ships, as seen from the air, although a small group compared to later standards, was an awe- inspiring sight.

I was always surprised when the ships came into view; navigation was such an art. I never dreamed that one day ordinary people would see the same, even from photographs and cinema film. Who would have thought that a time would come when ordinary people would fly three or four times higher, three or four times faster, without freezing, and oxygen in a pressurized cabin.

Although I was lucky enough to mainly experience uneventful operations while flying out of Calshot on the Solent (between the Isle of Wight and Southampton), it was on my third or fourth operation out into the Western Approaches that we spotted a Junkers

88, a German fighter/bomber. No one had seen one this far out into the Atlantic, and they were becoming more aggressive. He didn't hesitate and swept in on our starboard side. He passed over—or under—us at an impossible angle for me to use my gun effectively. Nevertheless, I let go a long burst just in case, while the fore and aft guns were blazing away. The Junkers hit us a number of times from midship to the tail area and continued to fly east and quickly out of sight.

I became aware of considerable amount of blood splatter all around me and saw our starboard gunner slumped in his bracing strap that normally supports the gunner as he manipulates the heavy machine gun. It was a horrific sight for me. I can't recall his name, but it was something like Billy Brown or Tommy Thompson. He had been hit straight in his chest, but the exit wound in his back was huge and covered the fuselage interior with blood and other human tissue. I immediately added to the mess by being violently sick—I was not yet 19. The tail gunner and I unclipped Billy (or

Tommy) from the gunner's support strap and laid him out near the tail. We flew on to meet our convoy, very shaken and very apprehensive indeed. The stores replaced my heavily soiled flying jacket on our return, but nothing has ever erased the memory or terror I felt at the first real casualty of war that I experienced. I have often thought that but for Timothy's aide-mémoire, regarding port and starboard, it well could have been me lying near the tail of our Sunderland

There were many occasions when flying boats came back seriously damaged with casualties on board. One "boat" came back with its hull so seriously damaged that it was in danger of sinking when it touched down on the Solent surface. The pilot beached it directly on our launch concrete slipway. It had been jumped by three Junker 88's. Several of the crew suffered severe wounds, and I seem to recall there was one fatality aboard.

The routine went on steadily, I helped Cyril with armaments, and he'd try to help me with Morse, but it was hard for me, very hard indeed.

One weekend, I decided I'd like to go to

London but there were no passes. I opted to take a chance and go without one. I arranged for mates to answer for me on the Sunday church parade, but I actually ducked out of camp Saturday afternoon. I went to Southampton on the public bus and brazenly bought a rail ticket to London. I was not challenged by any of the M.P.s who could, and did, demand of any serviceman proof of his leave pass— which I obviously did not have! Mother was already in Harwich, so I went to see Marjorie, who was my girl at the time. (She later on sent me a "Dear John" while I was overseas and ultimately became a G.I. bride.) We went to the pictures, and afterwards, I went back to the Y.M.C.A. in Paddington to stay overnight. I guess I was with Marjorie about the same time the lads were answering my name on the Sunday church parade back in Calshot. However, all good things come to an end, and it was soon time for me to return.

I boldly caught the train back to Southampton only to be met by a German air raid there. All hell let loose. As I got off the train, I was grabbed, with all the other airmen, sailors and soldiers, by the redcaps and directed to rubble clearing. Of course, no one asked for my leave pass. Eventually I started to walk back to Calshot, a good fifteen miles away, but as I got out onto the Farley road, one of our lorries came along, so I thumbed a lift. Getting in the back, I was shocked to find it full of the Calshot Military Police who had been on duty in Southampton. As the lorry stopped at the guardhouse and they all went inside, I slipped away, congratulating myself at being so lucky. I had been remembered though, and the next day I was charged with being out of camp since Church Parade without a pass. The C.O. was sympathetic and gave me a week on his garden. What with the regular cups of tea sent out to me by the C.O.'s wife via her maid (in the garden shed), it wasn't too bad considering what I would have got if I had been picked up on Waterloo station by the red-caps.

One afternoon shortly afterward, the Sergeant M.P. came into the library looking somewhat flushed and barked at me, "Well, what 'ave you been up to now?"

I remember jumping up and guiltily

saying, "Why, nothing Sergeant."

"Well," he said, "I have an officer asking for you. Come on!" As I walked into the guard-room, I saw my father standing there, resplendent in his blue Royal Marine best dress with red epaulets on his collar. He looked like the Director-General. I saluted him smartly.

Timothy gently asked the M.P. Sergeant if he could talk to me outside. "He's my son you see."

There was no objection. As I recall, my father just asked me if everything was okay. He had actually come to make his peace with me. He hinted that he was going away soon, wished me well, and shook my hand. I saluted him and he returned the salute. He then walked to the gate to the waiting Humber staff car that had brought him. I gave him another salute as the car turned past me on its way out, which he acknowledged with a little wave. It was all 'stiff upper lip' stuff, bred into both of us through years of Royal Marine tradition. He was second in command of the R.M. contingent that went into French North Africa to relieve the French of things they might have let the Germans have. That was his little "away" project. Our paths actually crossed during the war, although we never met, as this narrative will show. It was to be close on five years before I saw him again. My stock, however, improved immensely with all and sundry, dating from the time of the Royal Marine Officer's visit!

In the main, the days went fast in Calshot but how I hated Wednesday afternoons. It was the day we had to do Physical Training followed by 90 minutes of football; all in all a very hectic afternoon. It was good for us, they said! Then I discovered Cross Country running. Run the seven mile course, and you can go into the shower. Great! Within the hour, I'd had my shower. But I got so good at it that I was selected for the RAF Calshot Cross Country Team. Now I was running on Saturdays and Sundays, as well as Wednesdays, against the Southampton Police, the Navy from Portsmouth, and the Army from Poole. In fact, anyone who was prepared to challenge our accursed P.T. instructor. I often longed to "break a leg" so that I could get back to the guns,

Morse code, and the library but no such luck!

But the routine of Calshot was to be disrupted. Cyril was posted off to Blackpool for the first part of his wireless course leaving me in Calshot; I didn't expect ever to see him again. But within a fortnight, I was in Blackpool myself, getting ready for the Initial Wireless School with some trepidation. I learned the basic Morse code in the Winter Gardens and practised, hour upon hour, theoretically improving in speed at a rate of one word per minute per week. The weekly test was taken in the dance school, situated over a Burton's shop, a large pre-war men's outfitting emporium. It was fitted out with cubicles, desks, earphones, and note pads. Down the hall, the instructor—or sender—sat on a dais behind a desk in splendid isolation, sending the Morse that we tried to receive correctly.

I caught up with Cyril on the Blackpool front one day; a familiar face amongst the thousands of "rookie" airmen that swarmed the town. We were so pleased to see each other; one would have thought we'd been parted for years. Although we were in different squads and classes, we managed to spend most of our free time together. On several occasions, we went to the Blackpool Tower Ballroom dancing, but the fellows outnumbered the girls a dozen to one. Anyway, I always seemed to have two left feet when it came to dancing. Cyril, however, was quite a ladies' man on the dance floor. One weekend, we went to his home in Shirley where I met his sister Berenice for an hour or so before she left us to meet a boy friend. I didn't see her again until after the war, and then I married her.

I continued to struggle with Morse code, becoming more depressed with it as time went by. To fail your Morse test, which was taken in Burton's, gave rise to the raff slang "going for a Burton", a soft way of saying getting "the chop" or being dead. The system allowed for one speed failure, then you were put back a week, to do the same speed again, and failure then meant

SWORDFISH
Single engine (Torpedo) Reconnaissance Bi-plane
Wing span 45 ft. Length 36 ft.
Armament : One 0.303" Lewis or Vickers machine gun on a Scarff ring
Crew : Pilot, Air gunner

"out." I went for my dreaded "Burton" at nine words a minute: I was utterly desolate that I'd failed. The same week, Cyril passed his eleven words per minute speed and went on to the advanced wireless school at Yatesbury in Wiltshire.

I never saw Cyril again, although we wrote regularly to each other until he was shot down in the Far East. From a Wireless Operator, he had re-mustered to Observer, and after flying in Lancasters over Europe, he was posted to India as an Observer flying in Mosquitoes. He was shot down by the Japanese near Ramlee Island, and languished in Rangoon jail for some months, before dying of malaria.

After my failure with the wireless course, I went before a re-muster panel, which decided I was a qualified L.A.C. Air Gunner. They would  send me to Lytham St. Annes, a small pre-war private airport just south of Blackpool called Squires' Gate. Coastal

Command had some old modified torpedo Swordfish aeroplanes there, carrying half a dozen 100-pound bombs under the wings and room for a pilot and gunner/observer. Our task was to patrol the Irish Sea (see map page 38) around the Isle of Man, down to Fishguard (South Wales), and back again to spot any German submarines. U-boats were virtually invisible from the surface, but from above, owing to the relatively shallow sea, they showed up like whales against the sea bottom when the light was favourable. I flew with a great chap, a Flight Sergeant Tubby Brookes, and that brief time was the most pleasant of all my time in the RAF. We were looking for enemy submarines—not that we ever saw any in those home waters. I use to question what offensive action we could take other than strafe a surfaced boat. We carried nothing more lethal than me and my Vickers gun and some 100-pound bombs. I often doubted what use we were, but one kind naval person remarked that our very presence deterred the enemy. I wonder! It became "stand-down" before long when the Defiants started to arrive, and I went back to the re-muster panel. The training organisation of the RAF was becoming more sophisticated and geared to standardisation. The number of men handled was such, that if you were out of step, it was impossible to restart in the middle of a course. I tried to become a photographer but there were no vacancies at the time, so I took a Despatch Rider course, meaning to remuster later.

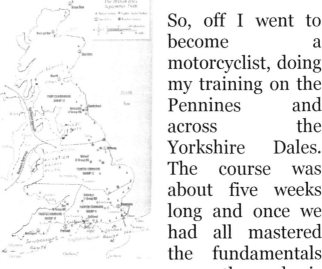

So, off I went to become a motorcyclist, doing my training on the Pennines and across the Yorkshire Dales. The course was about five weeks long and once we had all mastered the fundamentals on the basic training ground, we were off to the hills. Half a dozen motorcycle trainees would follow the instructor like a school of crocodiles, over the toughest terrain the instructor could manage with his three-wheeled combination outfit. The bikes were not very well treated by us lads. Each time a bike broke down, the rider would leave it for a WAAF (a girl trainee driver) out of Weedon to collect it with a lorry. It was funny to see the fourth or fifth rider trying to get a place on the sidecar outfit because no-one wanted to be left with a broken down machine (You might not get back to camp for hours!) Halfway through the course, the machines were upgraded. We knew we were in for some real hard work when the instructor appeared mounted on a high-powered solo motorbike. Some of the mountain routes must have been planned with a degree of spite, designed to break man or machine or both. After a long day being jarred to death on boulder strewn tracks, fording not too shallow streams, and footing through mud holes, often in very inclement weather, the sign to return to base was more than welcomed by us weary, rookie Despatch Riders. In retrospect, it was all good fun, and I felt I had accomplished something when I passed out. I came to terms with the fact that I had changed my flying jacket for a different type of specialised uniform: my D.R. boots and a Smith & Wesson .38 revolver.

Within a month, I was posted to 11 Group (Fighter Command) to a station in Kent called Hawkinge. The station was situated quite close to the coast, just north of Folkestone, and was subjected to a number of strafe type raids. Just before dusk one evening, I was returning back to base, which was situated in a huge hanger. As I approached, I became aware of a fighter coming in low and fast across the field. Flashes and sparks were emanating from its wings. It was shooting into the hanger. There was extensive damage to equipment in there but no casualties, luckily the hanger crew had just gone off duty. Thirty seconds later, I would have been in there. Another, 'What if.'

The airfield suffered an occasional unexplained explosion and it was rumoured that a shell from a huge German gun had been fired from across the Channel.

For a couple of months, I was part of a number of D.R.s who were like a pony express, running day and night in mainly foul weather it seemed, between the various fighter stations in West Malling, Biggin Hill, and Manston. It had taken me nearly a year to get here, but before I settled down, I was on the move again.

This time it was an overseas posting.

CHAPTER FOUR

GROUNDED BUT AT SEA

THE OVERSEAS POSTING GAVE ME leave to say good-bye to my mother in Harwich and to my girl-friend, Marjorie, in London. From Hawkinge in Kent, I was sent to Cardington once again, this time for completely new equipment including all manner of tropical gear. Thence by train to Greenock in Scotland and, in due time, I found myself on a beautiful ship called the *Athlone Castle*. It was a well-fitted cruise liner that had not been gutted. I shared, with two others, a cabin situated at the stern above the water line. We lay at anchor in Greenock Sound for many days and life became a little tedious.

One night we quietly moved out, and by daybreak, we were surrounded by sea and ships, all on the move. I had no duties and spent hours hanging over the back rail, watching the vortices produced by the propellers. It got colder and colder by the day. We were obviously going north and had several days of extremely bad weather. Everyone was very ill. I can't say how high the waves were but they towered over the ship at times, and we seemed all alone in the cold vastness of the ocean.

The days went by and the weather improved. It got steadily warmer, and on one sunny afternoon, a target balloon was released. Every gun on every ship, big and small, had a go at it. The noisy guns, fixed on the *Athlone Castle's* stern, seemed to jolt the whole ship as it joined in the general melee. Puffs of smoke appeared in all quarters of the convoy and way up in the sky. The excitement and noise created by the exercise, which went on for quite some time, caused the adrenaline to flow. However, I was not reassured to watch the balloon slowly drift away, out of sight, unscathed by all the steel that was thrown at it.

The weather got warmer still, and then we were suddenly outside Freetown on the West African coast, greeted by millions upon millions of mosquitoes, which attacked us regardless of our anti-mosquito cream. Then down we went to the Equator to be shaved and ducked by "Neptune" in the ship's open-air swimming pool and presented with a certificate afterwards. It was on this ship I was introduced to Crown & Anchor—a banned navy game—and lost every penny I owned. I never, ever gambled again!

The days went by pleasantly enough, although I wondered, yet again, if the war would be over before I got into it. I needn't have worried. One bright day, the ships moved into line astern, and on the horizon appeared a town with a New York skyline; it was Durban, South Africa. We docked at last and were given shore leave. I was very pleased to be handed a ten-shilling note because I was penniless. In the event, it did not matter because the whole of the dock road was filled with cars collecting airmen and soldiers to sample the hospitality of South African homes. I have memories of sumptuous meals in cool bungalows, of being waited on by lots of young blacks, of crickets making a deafening row as the sun went down, of long cool drinks and clean white sheets. I also remember the poor, poor blacks who hastened to get out of your way as you walked the main shopping streets, and of the hateful tolerance of the 'Boer' South Africans who resented the 'English' very much.

Back on the *Athlone Castle* we learned that we were to trans-ship, and there was a great deal of hectic activity. The packing of kit bags, endless queuing, endless waiting, calling of names and numbers, marching through the docks until we finally stood under the great hulk of the *Ile-de-France*, a ship many times the size of the *Athlone Castle*.

Thousands of soldiers and airmen had converged from smaller ships and as we struggled up the gangway, every fiftieth man or so was given a tag. Little did I know the agony and sweat that tag would mean for me. It transpired that I had been given mess duty, which meant working in the galley non-stop sixteen hours a day. There were four sittings for every meal, and as one meal finished, the next began. What with my sweat, and that of others, dripping into the soup caldrons, and the cockroaches, which were everywhere underfoot, I hardly ate a thing whilst on board.

On board the ship, we were ushered, like a never-ending line of moving kit bags, down below the decks to find that the ship had been gutted of all its fittings. Huge, cold bare iron caverns greeted us. From the rusty paint-peeling ceilings, long stalks of iron were fixed, each carrying a couple of large hooks, reaching down to about shoulder height. They looked like a forest of evenly spaced stalactites. It was from these hooks that each man's hammock was to be suspended.

Once out of Durban and on the high seas, we were subjected to numerous lifeboat drills. Being heavily engaged with the galley routine, I was only caught once in a drill exercise. From my hammock area deep in the heart of the ship, it took me the best part of an hour to follow the slowly moving snake of men up the stairwells to the upper deck. Even then, I never found my correct lifeboat colour! I quickly formed the opinion that there would be little chance of getting out if the worst should happen. I don't know how many men there were on the ship—five, ten, maybe twenty thousand—but between decks it was possible to touch another man by just stretching out an arm. I found myself sleeping in the galley, in spite of the cockroaches, (something my mother would never have believed, considering my morbid fear of crawly things). Rather that, than going down to the claustrophobic trap of the ship's interior.

The huge *Ile-de-France* was a very fast ship, and we steamed alone up the Indian Ocean into the Gulf of Aden and through the Red Sea to Port Tewfik and Egypt. From the great liner, anchored in the harbour roads, we were transferred by a string of picket boats to shore.

Gladly wishing the *Ile-de-France* to the devil, I landed amid the swirling dust of Tewfik, so glaring, so white, so sizzling hot!

CHAPTER FIVE

SALAD DAYS IN THE DESERT

ON AN ASSORTMENT OF LORRIES, we bumped along dusty roads amid the noise and smells of a foreign culture heading north along the Suez Canal treaty road to the junction of the two Bitter Lakes, a place called Kabrit. The word means "match" but became more like matchless or infamous. Kabrit was a peace-time aerodrome built on a spit of sandy land separating the two Bitter Lakes of the Suez Canal.

We thought we were fortunate to be allocated the permanent huts as sleeping

Front row. Flossie, me, John - 2nd to my left.

quarters on our first night on the station and cheerfully settled in.

The only real difference between a Home base station and Kabrit appeared to be the muggy climate and the mosquito nets shrouding the iron low slung beds. Hardly were the lights out when there was an audible scratching and rustling which was hard to identify. Odd matches were struck here and there, odd oaths and expletives arose; then the lights went on. The whole floor was one seething mass of insects and beetles the like of which I had never seen! But the real horror was the bed bugs inside the mosquito nets we had over us! Some of us retreated to the veranda but the bugs pursued us. Finally, another chap and I made our way to the M.T. garage and with one blanket under and one over we lay on the concrete floor.

The other chap was John Jones (Jonah), and we became firm friends, comrades-in-arms for four years, and after the war, each other's best man.

Kabrit was regularly shot up by the Luftwaffe and they usually came in twos and threes, very fast and very low. The layout of the camp was obviously well known to friend and foe alike. However, we all reckoned that the very large and colourful signs giving directions to the Armoury, Bomb Store, and M.T. Workshops etc. were intended for the low flying Jerry airmen who might be new at the job! Before the raids became too serious, John and I used to collect unopened beers abandoned on the N.A.A.F.I. tables by the faint-hearted. We became known as the Sneaky Stella Stealers.

One of the most unpleasant memories I have of the Bitter Lakes and Kabrit (and the most painful) is when about a dozen of us rushed down naked to the lake, jumping in to find the water a solid seething mass of jelly fish. We all got stung to some degree, but more than anything for me, it was the revulsion I felt for the slimy creatures.

One of the most pleasant memories was the day a wide-eyed mongrel bitch bounded into the camp, dodging the determined attempts of the guard on the perimeter gate to deny her access. John and I watched, with some amusement, at the single-mindedness of the little animal as she doubled back and forth to get her own way, ultimately making a bee-line to the Motor Transport Area where we were standing.

Flossie, as she became known, shared her time between John, the cookhouse, and me equally, except when she entertained Spot, the Commanding Officer's dog. Flossie was destined to become the grand dame of all the dogs we ever had in the squadron, in the Wings, and in the Group over the next four years. She had obviously belonged to a serviceman somewhere, someone associated with transport, because there was something about petrol, oil, and sweat that attracted her like a magnet. She also had an unfailing desire for regular meals, which probably accounted for her shared affections with anyone associated with the cookhouse. But she was quite selective about her special friends—non-commissioned ranks only, cookhouse chaps with gifts of course, all transport drivers but particularly John and me.

In those first few weeks in Kabrit, when there was so much for us "new boys" to learn, it was Flossie's early warning system that endeared her to so many. Normally an air raid warning was only given when it was obvious that we were the target. Flossie's long ears told her more than the hesitant guesses of the official lookouts and ambiguous radar. With a howl, she would race to the soft sand and dig; and boy, how she would dig! She'd burrow deep and disappear before anything had fallen or the A.A. guns had opened up, and I quickly learned to follow her example.

We had had a bad week of harassment raids from Jerry and had lost some lorries around the camp, so the transport officer decreed that the vehicles would be dispersed out in the "blue" or desert. That night the lorries were placed out in a great circle, some two or three miles out from the camp. In the morning, we discovered that a number of the lorries, out of the fifty or so, were sitting on piles of sand and all the wheels were gone! The local Egyptian villains had removed them, collecting a wondrous price no doubt, for their ingenuity and enterprise, in the main cities of Ismalia and Cairo. The camp police organised everyone into armed search parties, and we systematically combed the area for miles around, but it was a complete waste of time and effort. Experience was to prove, time and time again, that the ordinary "felon" was a better thief than anyone would give him credit. For those who have so little, it is a way of life, and who can blame them?

The first time true, gut-aching fear gets you is an experience that sets a pattern for a life-time. The source of the fear matters little. It's the realisation that it exists and generates in circumstances that are of little or no consequence to another, but is so earth shattering to you.

I don't exaggerate when I say that events in my life which would have shocked me into utter immobility in the early days, later passed almost without notice, with barely a shrug. I still remember the fear, the soul-racking fear of that particular night in Kabrit! And yet, I cannot say why it was so.

An air raid by a lone raider. He came over and dropped his bombs but as we went to help the injured, he swept low and machine-gunned us. We scattered, and as I ran as if the devil were after me, I lost a shoe. My foot was being torn to shreds by the gritty ground, but I couldn't stop. When I did, the best I could do was to bleat "my shoe" as though I expected some other chap would go back to it for me, for I could not! I can still physically taste that fear. I had a lot to learn. About war. About men. Most of all, about myself!

In the early days of the war, particularly in the Middle East, things were still run on peace-time lines, especially in Kabrit on the junction of the two Bitter Lakes on the Suez Canal. All things were done according to KRR (Kings Rules &

Regulations) "If it moves salute it, if it doesn't then whitewash it." My buddy, John Jones, was an aircraft engine fitter who was acting as a motor fitter, and I was a Despatch Rider. We often missed breakfast because somehow we never managed to get to the mess tent in time, usually owing to the fact that we never seemed to get up early enough. Then we discovered the "chit"! Providing one had a chit, one could get anything. John and I took turns signing each other's chits for all sorts of things, particularly for late breakfasts. It worked for months before we were sent into the desert, and the war proper and chits no longer had any meaning.

The early part of 1941 had seen the victorious British forces, though heavily outnumbered, ousting the Italians out of Cyrenaica (modern Libya). However, the Germans injected some of their units into the North African theatre of operations. That proved to be enough to swing the balance against the relatively small British army, who had to retreat out of their newly acquired territory. It was a war of swift movement, and the battle lines were not clear cut or defined, rather more like the boundary between oil and water when disturbed. It was a regular seesaw, usually referred to as the "Matruh Races" by the soldiers and airmen there, indicative of the rush back to the base camps.

The enemy consisted mainly of Italians, with a stiffening of German troops here and there. As time went by, the ratio of German to Italian increased as the Afrika Korps, under General Rommel, asserted itself. It wasn't the Italians or Germans we had to beat, it was Rommel. He was bold, brilliant, efficient, and the embodiment of all good things German: occasionally impulsive and highly respected by all and sundry, especially by us! Rommel took control of the battle from the hands of the Italian Marshals, to whom he was originally subordinate. The British effort lacked a certain continuity because it ran under a series of Generals, namely Wavell, Auchinleck, and lastly

Alexander (Montgomery being subordinate to Alexander).

But in 1941, events in the Western Desert were being influenced by many other outside factors, other than the awesome strength of the combined Axis Powers relative to the British "thin red line." Nevertheless, Malta was proving to be a thorn in the side of the enemy, who discovered that the Mediterranean was not the "Mare Nostrum" (Our Sea) that the Italians had always claimed. It was getting more difficult for them to move supplies across the inland sea. But it was even more difficult for England, who had to use the long way around the Cape of Good Hope, the South African route. Material was finding its way to Egypt from the States—carried in British ships, of course—since the U.S.A. was not yet in the war.

We were in a state of flux, moving men and munitions as best we could, first to plug this gap and then that one. I became part of a squadron formed from the ground staff available in the Canal Zone at that time (1941). Some Wellington bomber aircraft in Malta, on a short tour of operations, were directed to Egypt, instead of returning to England as the crews had expected. They were somewhat disgruntled to find themselves in Kabrit. There was a certain imbalance of trades and skills in the newly formed squadrons, for there was not the same range of personnel on hand in the Middle East Command as in the Home Command back in England; it was a case of "do and make do." This imbalance was to have repercussions for me later.

The first time the squadron officially went into the desert (usually referred to as the "blue"), we rookies new to the desert thought we were really defending Britain's lonely outposts. We had only been pitched for a couple of days when we were ordered to raise camp and re-pitch our tents on the other side of the miserable little tarmac road, which seemed to come from nowhere on its way to nowhere through the gritty barren countryside. We couldn't understand why, but the C.O. had discovered that the road was a boundary and the south side of the miserable little road was rated as "desert" and entitled all to fresh Desert

Rations (when available), and being so near base, they were available. It is just one of those things that the farther into the "blue" one goes, the less chance one is going to get fresh rations. However, here we were getting fresh meat, sweet potatoes, and bread (with weevils, of course) instead of bully beef, dried yak, and biscuits.

The C.O. was rated "tops." His name was Montgomery (no relation to the General who had not been heard of by desert folk in those days). He had a wonderful way with him and was liked by everybody. He demanded and got a salute first thing in the morning, accompanied by an accolade of "Good morning, sir" to which he would reply "Good morning corps, Bill, Brown or Merry", whatever was appropriate. For the rest of the day, he would just be around, and one could ignore his rank. One would find him head in engine with a fitter, scrounging a cup of tea in a tent, asking why something in the motor pool was being done the hard way because there's a tool for it (and if not it would appear in a week from somewhere). To everyone's despair, he went down in flames over Benghazi one night, and the whole squadron went into mourning. We felt as though we had lost the war.

The Squadron moved forward a little way to a Landing Ground known only as L.G.106. It took a couple of days to settle in, cooks organising the cookhouse, armourers sorting out the bomb stocks, the M.T. section bringing in additional supplies, etc., and all was made ready for night bombing operations. After a week, the slick efficiency and readiness of the squadron was there for all to see. There was little for me to do as our Wing and Group organisations were close at hand, and communication lines were short. I was quite intrigued, when on Daily Routine Orders, there was a request for airmen with photographic knowledge to report to the Adjutant. I had wanted to train as a photographer before I became a D.R., but it had been denied me. I now realised that I enjoyed the freedom and challenges that the D.R. position offered. Nevertheless, I'd always been keen on photography, ever since I had received a Box Brownie camera at a Royal Marine boys' Christmas party when I was about eleven, so I went to see what it was all about. The choice for the Adjutant was limited, as I was the only candidate. The squadron had a large lorry-sized photographic trailer full of aircraft cameras. The armoury had stocks of the four-feet-long, several million candle power magnesium air flashes, but we had no photographers. My instructions were simple. "Here are the manuals, the C.O. would like some cameras in the air in a week. Go!" After a few days I had the gist of fitting the cameras and processing the films, and though we were bombing Benghazi at the time and all seemed fine, the developed films proved to be unsatisfactory. There simply was no result.

I should briefly explain how night cameras work. The film is five inches wide, and the picture is five inches square. There is no shutter on the camera (it's for night photography). A control operates so that when the bombs are released, the huge air flash is dropped some seconds after the bombs have gone. A new unexposed piece of film is automatically advanced into the gate just before the air flash explodes, illuminating all below. Once the flash explodes, the picture it has taken is wound safely into the magazine. The only snag was that the aeroplane had to fly straight and level after the bombs had gone! Nasty. Especially if the natives below are hostile. Regardless of our best efforts on the ground, the results we were getting in the air were clearly unsatisfactory. On being quizzed by the C.O. and the Intelligence Officer, I re-stated how essential it was to fly straight and level after the bombs had gone. Subsequently the C.O. told me to fix a camera in his aircraft for the next run, and he was sure I would like to go with him to ensure correct operation. It was a hair raising experience to "go in" at way under ten thousand feet with all that flak about, to do what these chaps were doing night after night, at a time when only one crew in four survived a tour of 30 "ops." We came back with a super picture of Benghazi harbour, and the C.O. was pleased, but there must be a better way to get pictures of target accuracy! And some of the crews were of the same mind; they would press home their attack with vigour but did not relish stooging around steadily afterwards just for a picture!

Before long, the squadron moved forward again, and I reverted to being a Despatch Rider. At about the same time, we had a couple of photographers join us from the Delta pool. This was when I started to carry a camera, which I used to photograph the war scenes and produce pictures of our various squadron personnel. Later, in co-operation with the photographic people, we ended up selling sets of pictures to the lads on the

---

An Aside

When I was in Italy in 1945, my mother sent me a little booklet, which she thought would be of interest to me about the RAF Ground Crews in Tripolitania. It cost one shilling and nine pence and was published by the Stationery Office. The two pictures across the first pages were of some of my squadron lads on the back of a couple of our lorries and were, no doubt, pictures taken by me on one of our convoy moves.

---

unit.

The landing ground at Daba, separated from the coast by a narrow tarmac road and a single railway line, hugs the coast and the coast road where-ever possible. The easiest crossing point was at Tel el Eisa, between Daba and a small railway halt called El Alamein; a place destined to be included in all war history books for the battle that would one day take place there.

One glorious afternoon, I had been up the road to visit a neighbouring Squadron to meet Leslie Charteris (the author of The Saint book series,) who was one of the aircrew flying Wellington bombers at that time. We spent several hours talking about the art and craft of story telling; how he had invented a large number of characters before dreaming up "The Saint." I was at peace with the world as I rode back pondering, among other things, that apart from talent, one has to have an idea, when the whole of the road in front of me was full of sparks, sweeping in a great arc away from me. I threw myself and the bike off the road in utter disbelief. That swiftly disappearing speck on the horizon—the swine, could you believe it, he'd fired at me. Me! A single despatch rider alone on a desert road! (A practice we followed later and especially in Europe after D-Day. In fact, anything that moved was strafed, and historically, Rommel was badly injured by this method in Europe after the North African campaign.) As I picked myself up, I realised I'd heard nothing!

Sometime later I was subjected to a similar attack, but I felt that it was much more justified and certainly less personal. I went with the Water Bowser driver to Hammett Well to collect the squadron's daily water supply, and on the way  back I asked if I could drive. This was to be the first time I had ever driven a four-wheeled vehicle, and I was quite looking forward to the experience. We had had an accident free, non-eventful journey back we thought, only to find no water in the water tank because it was full of holes! I (we) had been strafed yet again. Incredible as it may seem, neither of us had heard or felt a thing—not that one could hear much with that huge engine in the cab—but even so! The only other time I drove the Water Bowser, I was with John and came off the tar-mac road into the camp track much too fast, hitting a series of "humps", which resulted in fracturing the tank and losing the all the water again. No one would let me near the Water Bowser after that!

My drinking companion in this picture was run down one night and unfortunately killed by one of our own lorries near Kairouan, Tunisia a year later.

I was never one who could stack pints of beer away and remain upright. I would invariably go to sleep, usually before the robust singing started or any of the small fights broke out. I have been known to slip under the mess table and arise refreshed, sometime later, to rejoin my friend John still busily sinking them back. More than once, John has stepped out from the mess tent into the crisp night desert air to find me comfortably asleep under the starlight at the bottom of a slit trench, where I had fallen with the grace of an acrobat. Whenever John and I went back to Cairo for a few days leave, he would go "up market" and drink whisky—his favourite tipple—and I would try a brandy or two.

One bright and cheery morning, I had to go to the RAF H.Q. in Cairo with an Intelligence Report. Even though John and I were going into Cairo that evening because we had scrounged an overnight pass, he still asked me to bring him back a hip bottle of whisky. I did the round trip to the H.Q. and back but found no sign of John in our communal tent on my return. I recall idly wondering what the unknown brand of whisky tasted like. John found me flat out on his bed, still in my full D.R. kit. I have heard it said that he was livid! However, I came to propped up against the Kursaal Bar in Cairo, dressed in my dusty "best blue." No mean feat when one realises that with the help of some mates, I'd been carried several hundred yards to my tent, redressed, shaved, bundled into a lorry, driven into Cairo and lifted onto a bar stool to come round in my own good time.

John and I regularly used to go deep into the desert interior to see what we could find, and some very interesting times we had. Originally, John had a clapped out old British bike but he did acquire a German Flat Twin motorbike from one of our expeditions. Miles out in the blue, we came across a deserted German airfield. It was complete with damaged Stukas, some immobile Italian lorries, a few odds and ends of small German vehicles, and a couple of motorbikes, one with a sidecar attached. There were hundreds of other things, rifles and ammunition, batteries, and countless desirable Jerry cans; it was our very own Aladdin's Cave for weeks. We had to look out for booby traps, some of which were not to easy to see, like charges inside petrol tanks connected to the caps and on door swings. There were all sorts of trip wires laid just an inch below the sand surface. John eventually got both bikes running. He used one, and the Engineering Officer gave John a fiver for the other. John also ran a "peoples car"—one of Hitler's specials—a very small four-seater, which we called the

Sand Boat.

One particular day John was not free to come scrounging with me, so off I went alone. As usual, I went along the coast road until, quite at random, I turned south into the blue of the desert. I zigzagged my way from one mark (a burnt out tank or vehicle) to another. I had probably been away from the camp for three or four hours and was about thirty or thirty-five miles from the coast road, when my motorbike petered out. It was a 498cc B.S.A. side valve with a rubber pipe connecting the fuel tank to the carburetor. The pipe had fractured, losing all my remaining petrol. So there I was, an impossible distance from the coast without water. I remember sitting in that gully, smoking cigarettes and cursing my stupidity for being so unprepared, for I surely should have known better. This was to prove to be the real beginning of my survival experience. I was in a pretty desperate situation and I knew it. Then I could hardly believe my ears, a motorbike. Then I could hardly believe my eyes as over the ridge came John! One can't calculate the odds;

becoming free, John had decided to go out on the scrounge too. He just went "out and about" in the vastness of the desert and, by pure chance, came upon me. He towed me back with a loose rope, but afterwards, we never went out alone and never without a spare water bottle.

It's surprising how many bottles of beer one can consume without actually counting. We had had a regular camp for a couple of months, and in consequence, we had collected quite a store of empties. They were placed in a small hole by the side of our tent, and the obliging, gently moving sand had covered them up. Then one night we had a sand blow. The wind was hot and stifling; the tent quickly filled with swirling dust, which matted the hair, filled one's nose and ears, and blocked the corners of the eyes. Several times during the night, we had to go out to ease the weight of sand off the lee side of the tent. That was the first time I learnt to wear a gas mask as an aid to breathing in a sand storm, in spite of the clammy feeling of wearing the accursed thing. The funny thing about these storms is that the sand is scooped out of one place to be piled up in another. When John and I emerged from the tent next morning, we were met by an evacuated bottle tip containing dozens of pristine beer bottles. On the returns to the N.A.A.F.I. mess tent, we had enough refund money for two full crates. Quite a windfall!

The day to day and night to night routine of air operations went on steadily: the maintenance schedules, the arming and refuelling, the photographic and other intelligence, the selection of targets, the briefing of the aircrews, the count of aircraft lifting safely off, the count of returning planes. The quiet realisation and sadness for friends not coming back, followed by the immediate necessity of getting on with the new days chores. It's an appalling thing to realise that at the time, out of 100-odd aircrew sitting in at a briefing session, 40 to 70 of them would be killed or missing within six weeks.

A sister squadron was situated a few miles up the road near Fuka, and one night they were raided by sea-borne Germans who, in the middle hours of the night watch, had come ashore and done a demolition job on some of the Wellington aircraft not on operations. They had then generally shot up the camp, causing untold confusion in the dark, and killing about fifteen of our chaps before getting away scot-free. There followed several other incidents up and down the coast, and for a while, we all were a little jittery and edgy until we came to terms with it and found an answer to the threat. After a while, squadrons near the coast were never unprepared for such attacks, but it became another chore to look to.

About a fortnight after the German sea-borne raid, our aircraft were diverted to a "satellite field" in the near desert because of heavy local sea mist on our own ground. In the early hours of the morning, we became aware of a heavy *crunch*. Through the night mist, there was a glow of something big burning, accompanied by the uneven crackle of small arms fire. We dove into our slit trenches, most of the chaps with rifles, me with my revolver. The firing was heavy but spasmodic; one or two of the blokes ran back to their tents, crouching low, to retrieve forgotten items such as tin hats, ammo clips, etc. I went back for a Sten gun (a simple machine gun) and later, for a blanket or two. I'm not kidding but it was a very long, cold night, full of tension but no Germans. Believe me, anyone or anything coming down the track unannounced, would have been met with a withering fire from many tense and trigger-happy airmen.

An hour after sun up, we discovered that the "firing" was, in fact, one of our own aircraft, which had crashed on landing. It was the machine gun ammunition exploding in the fire, which had quickly taken hold. We felt just a little sheepish, even if relieved. I seem to remember that we suffered a nasty rash of sand-fly bites on that particular night. There is a time in their life cycle when the flies actually burrow into the skin and leave some eggs behind. The bite then festers up, causing a nasty sore, which takes ages to heal and sometimes causing a severe fever.

John and I made friends with a guy who seemed a little different, and he was. Hicky was a "Battle of Britain" pilot, who had wanted a change from one kind of aircraft to another but was refused and finally marked down as L.M.F. (Lack of

Moral Fibre). A terrible injustice that he wore without flinching. On rare occasions, we would go back down to Cairo to get a bath, have a haircut and a comfortable shave, before going into the Kursaal Bar for drinks and a meal. And Hicky would "write some money" to pay the bill. For someone like me, who had never had a bank account, a cheque was the supreme novelty! Hicky's father was a pre-war diplomat stationed in Cairo for about ten years. Hicky was obviously pilot material who had let the side down! Hence, the L.M.F. tag! And all this brave lad wanted to do, remember, was to change from one kind of aircraft to another, but "it showed lack of confidence in the aircraft" etc.

Our forward troops were making good progress and had made new inroads into Cyrenaica beyond Fort Capuzzo and Bardia. As a D.R., I was attached to an Army Signals unit and went with a confirmation signal to a forward unit. Across the road, there were literally hundreds of Italian solders sitting on the verge, all very happy to be out of it all, loosely guarded by a handful of redcaps.

The officer in charge of signals told me to help move the prisoners back to Stage One cages because he wanted them off his site! The area was, if I remember rightly, about eight miles down the road. The objective was to move them down the road and not on it. I played the role of sheep dog, continually circling the huge crowd, always pointing eastward. They were very good-natured with me and cheered me each time I came around, but once we started to move, I never saw another British soldier until just short of Stage One. At Stage One, there were plenty of Red Caps and an Army Film Unit, who asked me to do my sheep dog act for the movie cameras—my first and only starring role! Anyway, I didn't hand over my charges to anyone, in case I'd lost one or two along the way. I'd been nearly ten hours looking after about five hundred Italians who'd had enough, and so had I. But I never worried because I was in complete command and I was well armed, I had my Smith & Wesson revolver and my standard issue of six rounds of ammunition!

There were times, of course, when I was

not so happy with the outcome and wished I were somewhere else. I had just collected a new Norton motorbike. It was probably one of the nicest bikes I'd had thus far, when I had occasion to be sent forward to a unit somewhere near Bardia. When I eventually found the unit, I was directed down to the Intelligence Complex, situated in deep square pits with sandbagged side walls and camouflaged nets with not much above ground level. While the Intelligence Officer was signing my release (a kind of receipt), there was an almighty explosion and dust flew everywhere from the sandy walls. My ears drummed and hurt, and I could hardly see. The I.O. had a trickle of blood from his nose, and my head felt as if it had been hit with a sledgehammer. The I.O. said with a splutter that they had been "dropping odd ones all day." Shells, he meant. When I went outside there was practically nothing to be seen of my new Norton motorbike, it had virtually disappeared. It had been blown to bits. The acrid smell of explosive was strong, but the I.O. took it all in his stride, not too concerned about the loss of my bike nor of the very near miss we had survived.

During the next two days, I was forced to stay there and endure many more near misses; it was generally very unpleasant. All forward areas worked under "C" stores system. Once you have taken whatever from the main issuing stores and signed for it, it was reckoned to be expendable. However, I knew questions would be asked. A D.R. coming back on foot looks a bit suspicious. However, the I.O., a strange man, gave me a note saying that my bike had been left there in an unserviceable state. In retrospect, it was his little joke.

It was during my enforced stay in the area I acquired a bed. My transport back to Daba included the bed. It was the envy of the whole M.T. section. Not for me, a stretcher on sticks or one made of 2 x 2 with its threat of bugs. I had a cast-iron bed with a history. It had originally belonged to an Italian Officer who had imported it from Italy, and I'm sure there was even more to it than that. However, I "met" the Italian in Capuzzo and he "gave" it to me without too much persuasion.

Being a D.R., my major problem was

always one of transport. I could hardly carry it on a bike whenever the squadron moved! I always had to bribe one of the drivers to load it on his lorry, and the bribe was usually to let him ride my bike for a while once in the new location. My problems disappeared when John became the main driver cum mechanic of the Fitters Wagon, which contained all the motor spares, tyres etc., and of course my bed!

Hicky, John, and I were going to try to arrange a kind of late Christmas dinner at the Kursaal, but before we could fix anything, Hicky was posted back to the Delta. However, before he left, we took him up the road to a sister squadron where he had friends. We were invited into their mess, and a party ensued. Coming back to our camp, we three sat in the front cab. John was driving, Hicky was in the middle singing loudly, and I was, well, leaning against a not too securely shut cab door. It could have been the swinging cab door that suggested I had "stepped out." At any rate, it appears that Hicky, in a hazy way, wondered where I had gone. John said he remembered putting me in the lorry. After some discussion, as they drove along, they decided to retrace their steps, as it were, and found me asleep in the sand by the roadside. Next morning, I only had vague memories of the night before and was quite puzzled at the excessive amount of sand in my hair.

Hicky went back to base, and eventually John and I went forward. John and I didn't get down to the Kursaal for our Christmas meal until way into the New Year, but when we did get there, we found it had all been paid for in advance. And Hicky? We never heard anything of him ever again!

The New Year of 1942 looked good. Benghazi had fallen to the British Eighth Army on Christmas Day, and we of the Desert Air Force were sweeping all before us. We heard with mixed feelings about Pearl Harbour, but we were saying, "Thank heaven for the Japs." At last, we are no longer alone! When Churchill received intelligence about Pearl Harbour, he immediately declared war on Japan, in the name of the British people, before even the Americans got round to it.

Some people sleep soundly, I am told, while others practically die. In my younger days, I qualified as a master in the latter class, representing a "peace of mind" I could hardly attribute to clean living and the good food of the desert! However, I used to have what we called a "one-man tent," and on this particular occasion, I had pitched it rather near to the runway. Following a session in the mess tent with John and some of the lads, I turned in once our aircraft had taken off for the night's target. In the morning, I hazily crawled out to find that one of our Wellingtons had come back with a hung-up bomb load. It had belly-flopped with folded undercarriage and bent props. It ended up not more than 100 yards from me and my tent. I grabbed my gear, boots, revolver and the rest, and jumping over the white tapes surrounding the bomber and me, raced across to John and Taffy's tent. They laughed themselves silly that I had slept through the commotion, the noise of the crash, all the excitement of the white tapes, and the rest. Taffy, who loved my D.R. gear, the boots, etc., picked up my revolver and after handling it for a while pointed it at the Wellington and pulled the trigger. At that precise moment, the delayed bomb load exploded. As we all instinctively fell to the ground, one could hear Taffy saying, "Christ!" I think he thought he'd done it!

My tent was blown away with all my personal kit, and my metal camping bed frame ended up a couple of hundred yards away. It suffered a bent leg, which was later repaired for me by the fitters. My bike was still standing by the mess tent where I had left it after boozing! But I had to smile at my good luck.

An Aside on Motorbikes

I guess I must have had a dozen bikes during my overseas service; each had its own "winsome ways," but the most solid and endearing bike was a B.S.A. 498cc side valve. Even though it had rubber petrol pipes, which used to fracture from time to time, and friction pads, which attracted sand, it seemed to go on and on. The old Webb link front forks suffered from a natural grinding paste created by the grease (needed to keep them working) and sand-dust, which resulted in a loose floppy action.

I once had two brand-new Royal Enfields within 20 minutes. I was going to scout for a 53 brand new lorry convoy from Port Tewfik at the south end of the Suez Canal to go to Bizerta at the north point of Tunisia.

From Ismalia Depot, I collected the new Enfield, and within a couple of minutes, I'd gone down into soft sand that hid a boulder. I was badly jarred and I had fractured the down tube of the bike frame. Within 20 minutes, I had a replacement Enfield and I was on my way. The 2000-mile run was a classic, and as a result, I received a "Mention in Despatches." It had to go to someone and there was only one D.R. and fifty-three drivers. If left to them, they would still be arguing about who should have it.

The bitchiest bike I ever had was a huge Harley Davidson, 750 cc, weighed at least 750 lb., foot boards, foot clutch, hand gear shift through a gate, sporting a broad based crankcase with only about a 3" ground clearance; and this for desert use! Times out of number, the wheels would sink in the soft sand, breaking the hard crust, causing the crankcase to ground. This would stop the bike dead allowing me to go sailing on. Invariably the engine would stay ticking over and the rear wheel would be gently spinning as the bike stood there upright. I'm sure it laughed at me at times but I didn't keep it long.

I had a beautiful Norton once, a famous pre-

war motorbike which I could never have afforded even if I'd have been old enough - pre-war - to have ridden one, but Jerry took exception to it and plonked a shell on it when I left it unattended outside an Intelligence *Officers dugout.*

I tried a side car outfit. There were a couple of snags, one was that I couldn't control where the sidecar would end up. At my first attempt, I flattened all the 'desert lilies' for some distance around. That meant re-digging the smelly things in again; they were old petrol tins set in the sand for ones convenience. The other snag was that if you weren't careful you could become a taxi.

At the time I was around Cassino, I had an A.J.S.; I didn't keep it long though because it suffered quite a lot of damage.

After Cassino, I had a 350cc Matchless, which was my all time favourite. It was lively and handled well in all the various situations I found myself. It was the longest serving member of my bikes and I had it until I came back to England. It was truly a riders' steed and you felt it was a part of you.

Chapter Six

IN THE FACE OF DEFEAT

ALTHOUGH IN JANUARY 1942 WE seemed to be doing so well, all our fortunes changed by February and, once again, the Army was having to retire against mounting German-Italian pressure. Malta, too, was going through a terrible time and because we had a detachment of our Wellington bombers going there for a specific task, we collected thousands of our free issue "VEE" cigarettes from all over the Group for the lads stranded there. Unfortunately, the whole operation was cancelled. One aircraft was still going anyway, and so it was loaded with all these cigarettes. They were packed everywhere, in the bomb bay and either side of the catwalk. I organised an unofficial trip with the crew as a passenger but it caused me more trouble than the pilot or I could possibly have anticipated.

We touched down at Luga at dusk and rolled off the runway taxiing towards the dispersal area when there was a vicious lurch. One of the Wellington legs had gone into a small bomb crater twisting it slightly and the prop was damaged too. It proved to be a miracle that the Wellington did not suffer anymore damage during the six days it lay in the open, after being pulled out of the hole, what with all the bombs and shrapnel falling about. The 'VEE' cigarettes were taken over by the Chaplain and I spent most of my time acting as an ammunition carrier and labourer for the A.A. gunners because I wasn't allowed off the aerodrome owing to my presence in Malta being 'unofficial'. I would be

AWOL (Absent Without Leave) when we got back, so I was naturally quite concerned!

The gallant fight of Malta is fully recorded in many of the war histories, but my world during those hectic six days was focused in an A.A. gun 3.7" gun pit. The noise and percussion of the gun, firing in that restricted space, battered your head and senses to a pulp after an hour or so. The inferno of the gun pit dulled the maelstrom of bombs and shrapnel that accompanied each lazy pass of the high flying enemy bombers in the clear blue sky. In between the raids, which were almost continuous, I worried that the Wellington might receive further damage, and I would have to stay in the gun pit forever! The army lads made me earn my keep as a "lugger" of this and that. "Lug that over here mate" was a phrase I learned to jump to.

Somehow, somewhere, by someone (bless the fitters), the Wellington was made serviceable again, and we got out of Malta safely. On landing back in Egypt, we found that we had had a change of C.O. and the whole episode was overlooked. It was not surprising. The first stage of a new "Matruh Race" was on—a retreat with all speed. There was no direct connection, of course, but while I had been away, our fortunes in the desert had suffered some reverses! From about the same position in Cyrenaica as our troops had reached the previous year, and had subsequently retreated under General Wavell, they were now forced to do the same again under General Auchinleck. I should try to put into perspective the distances over which these highly mobile battles raged. Whereas in World War I, losses and gains were often measured in yards and casualties in the hundreds of thousands. Ground lost and gained in the desert was often hundreds of miles, and while each casualty is someone's husband, father, son, or brother, the actual numbers were small compared with World War I.

The main battle ranged to and fro, over a distance of say, from London to Naples in a straight line - or halfway across the United States. From El Alamein to Tunis is nearly equivalent to, say, London to Moscow or three quarters of the distance across America. Once retreating, the pursued had to outrun the pursuer (hence the Matruh Races) to a prepared line. It wasn't quite that simple, but you get the idea. The first hold line was near Tobruk—the Gazala line. It held for several months, and then burst like a dam under increasing German-Italian pressure.

Tobruk fell. What a tremendous shock that was for us! Indeed, in the midst of a debate on future Anglo-American strategy, news of the fall of Tobruk was broken to Churchill by Roosevelt. Churchill said in his memoirs that it was one of the heaviest blows he could recall during the war. No reproaches were issued (from the Americans present), no unkind words spoken. (Remarkable when one realises that Churchill was pushing the preferred British strategy over the American preferred strategy at that time.) Roosevelt only asked what he could do to help.

There were all kinds of rumours about what was happening up front and our bombing targets seemed to change with uncoordinated rapidity. As a D.R., I heard dozens of different versions, but no one expected the headlong rush that ultimately took place. History shows that it was sketchily planned but for us at the time it was pure chaos. One night the usual pyrotechnics and near distant rumblings were rudely enhanced by tanks and trucks all barging through the main camp site. There were many hoarse shouts as through the night vehicles ploughed down tent ropes and rolled forward without much regard. All through the following day, the movement of heavies was noted from the slopes of Tel el Eisa, and it was all one-way traffic. In the darkness of the next night, the flashes and thunderclaps of big guns were nearer, and as the long night wore on, we reckoned that most of the Eighth Army had gone through. The early hours of the following day seemed very quiet. Some Kittyhawk fighter planes "dropped in," encouraged by our Wellington bombers, still on our field, that had some fuel and ammunition from us. We learnt that we were thin on the ground, and most of our people had moved back. Only a few vehicles were on the coast road. Those that were, were moving east. I went and visited a sister squadron near Fuka and found them breaking camp. On my way back I was shattered to see the main Daba Stores being set to the torch. There were enough rations stored there for an army; every conceivable delight in the way of cigarettes, beer; tons upon tons of tinned everything, peaches, cheese, condensed milk; everything imaginable; all being blown up and burnt.

Back on the squadron, the order was suddenly given to move. Everything that wasn't already packed was bundled into the lorries in haste and

the aircrew were instructed to take the Wellingtons back and land anywhere in the Delta. But we had one Wellington having an engine change and the crane driver had to stay with the pilot and fitters to finish the job. As D.R. I collected the convoy together and, at last, we were off heading east for Alexandria and the

Delta. During the remainder of that day and most of the night, we trundled on and on. I hadn't slept for more than a couple of hours over several days and sometime during the night, I eventually slipped in between two lorries of my fifty-odd vehicle convoy. The lorries inevitably bunched up and I 'came to' as I bumped off the tar-mac road onto the sand edge, only to realise that the whole convoy had stopped moving. (How far can one drive—or ride—in a hypnotic sleepy state?) The realisation that I had nearly become a 'self inflicted casualty' completely woke me up. By the time I had weaved to the Convoy Commander at the front of the line, it was all moving again. The tedious journey with the now strung out convoy, mixed with other vehicles all going into the Delta, ended when the Commander selected a spot for us to settle on the Treaty Road between Alexandria and Cairo. Our aircraft had congregated back at Kabrit on the Suez Canal. A day later, we moved the whole squadron ground crew back there too. To our relief the Wellington with it's new engine was safely back with the engine fitters on board, but of our crane driver there was no news at all, so I was instructed to do a search. I actually went all the way back to Daba, crossing the railway at Tel el Eisa, but there was no crane to be seen anywhere.

By noon, I was rolling noisily back to the Delta along the hot sticky road east over the depressing flat terrain. There simply wasn't a soul to be seen, no vehicles, no aeroplanes, absolutely nothing. I seemed to be the last person in the God-forsaken country. Then I saw a helmet, a head, a rifle, two heads, new wire and it dawned on me that I was going through a line. I also recall that I wondered how many of those army lads beaded their sights on me as I approached. In those days I wore a steel crash helmet which was very similar to the German pattern and I can only assume, now, that our chaps decided to let the stupid Jerry ride himself into the 'bag'. It would help to explain some of their surprise when they first took me in. Anyway, a little way along and I was waved to the side by menacing rifles and whipped smartly to an Intelligence Officer sitting in the usual sandbagged hole who could hardly believe that I had just come from Daba and was a 'Raff' D.R. to boot. "The road is cut by tanks, it's all Jerry out there etc." We never did see our mobile crane or driver again and we could only hope he was swept safely into a German prisoner of war cage.

GENERAL SIR WILLIAM JACKSON wrote in his book "North African Campaign 1940-43." of this time:

"During 29 June (1942) the desert between Matruh and El Alamein was covered with small columns of British and Axis vehicles all moving eastwards, trying to avoid each other.

Rommel turned the Afrika Korps off the coast road again at Fuka (Fuka, half a dozen miles west of Daba – and me!) *and advanced across the desert with little more than 40 tanks and 600 infantry, heading for the centre of the El Alamein Line. The 90th Light was hustled unmercifully from Matruh to head the Axis advance on the coast road.*

At midday on 30 June, it reported coming under heavy artillery fire near Tel el Eisa, a prominent hill on the south side of the coast road five miles west of El Alamein station.

The preliminaries of the First Battle of El Alamein had begun."

....which rather explains the surprise of my 'capturers' and it suggests that I was probably the last Brit out and back from that area at that time.

CHAPTER SEVEN

HOLDING ONE'S BREATH

THE EIGHTH ARMY ABSORBED THE shock of the Afrika Korps and held them in an area between the coast at El Alamein and a natural feature known as the Qattara Depression some thirty-odd miles inland. An escarpment leads down to the floor of the Qattara Depression, which is a low lying soft, salty, sea of sand; the surface of which will hardly bear the weight of a man. It is quite dangerous for even light vehicles and is an impregnable barrier for tanks and heavy guns. The Depression sweeps up diagonally from the deep desert, creating a natural bottleneck. It was here that the forward momentum of the Afrika Korps was dissipated, on a hastily prepared defence line, which was formed so desperately close to the Delta and the Suez Canal. Once forward movement is arrested, it is difficult to resurrect the initiative. Both sides continued to hurt each other in this semi-static situation. There were many set-piece battles in this area, while each side continued to strengthen its position where and how it could.

As an operating squadron, we had reformed back at Kabrit again. From there, our bombers were attacking targets in the forward areas. Our bombing line (a movable line on a map which denotes "bomb that side, it's them, but not this side, it's us") was barely a hundred miles away, although as a D.R. I was often very much closer than that. On most nights, there were seldom less that twenty flares floating down in the night sky and whole sections of the forward area would be illuminated under these candelabra. Continually there were red, orange, white and green tracer darting hither and thither like huge fire-flies accompanied by blinding flashes and deafening cracks and whooshes of nearby guns. Our bombing, by then, was so accurate that it was reputed to come right up to our own mine-fields, less than 2000 yards from our forward troops. This was the time of 'static movement'. We were all cramped into a relatively small area after experiencing the vast openness of the desert wastes.

There was, however, a regular run to an aircraft engine maintenance unit situated "safely" in Palestine. John managed to take it once as a perk (and some perk it turned out to be), and I went as his guard. We travelled across the Sinai Desert, in places a genuine picture postcard desert with drifting sand dunes. The lot, with a single soft tar-mac road threading its way across the wastes, occasionally disappeared. The road was a dusty sand colour, marred only by our tyre tracks, which followed us where the tar oozed up through the surface drawn by the passage of our lorry. Within minutes, the gently moving dust would stick to the moist tar and the road would return to its uniform greyness. We had to be on our guard from the 'natives' owing to the fact that because the Imperial British Army was suffering a defeat at the hands of the Germans etc., the English deserved no respect whatsoever. It was noticeable in the villages and towns, but particularly in Cairo, Alexandria, and Ismailia. The local felline were getting bold. They would make no pretence to stealthily relieve you of your valuables but rather would gang-mug (to use a modern term) if the opportunity occurred. So John had a rifle ready, and I had a stovepipe Sten automatic, as well as my normal revolver. You had to be wary not to let anyone board the vehicle from the tailboard or rear. It was essential to let everyone know as we passed through the village areas that we were fully awake, even though it often meant standing on the running board of the lorry. It was, as one would say, a hairy business. We exchanged our aircraft engines, collecting the new ones boxed in their crates just as they had come from England, and in due time started our return journey.

At odd places along the desert road, there were collections of 40 gallon barrels. To relieve the boredom of the run we stopped at one spot and selected a suitable barrel about a 1000 yards away to use as a target. After a few of shots each with Johns rifle, we drove up to it to see what we had done and were pleasantly surprised to find several hits on it but at the same time, unpleasantly surprised that from the holes, hot, sun roasted tar was cascading in a circle around the barrel's base. Somewhat guiltily, we drove on.

During the afternoon and without any warning, a wind raised the sand, and before long there was a full scale sand storm unleashed on us. The abrasive nature of a sand storm has to be experienced to be believed; at its most vicious, it will remove paint from a metal surface and embed grains in bare flesh. John and I were virtually trapped in the cab for a day and a half. Inside the cab, we were very miserable; gritty sand was everywhere, eyes, ears, nose, mouth, hair, just everywhere. We tried to make tea but it was out of the question, so we drank our warm, tinny tasting water. What with the gritty sand in our mouths, pouring tepid water into a mug with sand already in it, in the closed atmosphere of the cab full of swirling dust, the result was more like diluted mud! Eventually the storm subsided and it took us several hours to clear the banked up sand from the lorry side and from the inside of the engine compartment.

The effort of that sand shifting makes me remember the painful arm I had at the time. Relatively small abrasions and cuts take forever to heal in the desert especially if they are left without expert care and attention. I had chipped my elbow when I came off the bike some time previously, and to begin with, it formed a small circular scab. Whenever I changed the field dressing, I also took the top off and it left a progressively bigger hole each time. This was the makings of a 'desert sore' and it got a lot worse ending up at least an inch in diameter, before the medical officer beat the problem, but it has left a scar on my elbow to this day.

Suddenly it seemed as though the Canal Zone was getting very crowded. There appeared to be tank, gun, and vehicle parks springing up everywhere, though heavily camouflaged. However, there was something else—a new feeling of optimism and confidence seemed to be developing, even though we had only held on by our fingertips at El Alamein.

We were also all becoming aware of a certain General Montgomery.

CHAPTER EIGHT

THE LONG HAUL
(Westward Ho!)

I CAN'T CLAIM EVER TO have met him—General Montgomery, that is. He seemed to be avoiding me. He would turn up at a place the moment I left or he'd go somewhere before I had even been there; never-the-less, I had a close-up of his opening gambit on the 23rd October 1942. Not that I knew the date at the time!

Imagine, if you can, without any warning whatsoever, the most intense violent thunder storm breaking right over your head. It was as though God Almighty Himself was beating His Wroth down from the heaven! I was threading my way, in the semi-darkness, along a deeply rutted track when I was virtually blown off my 'bike as the world around me was torn asunder. I could now see, through screwed up eyes, the track outlined by the continuous flashes of the guns, while the viscous cracks and percussion battered my head and senses. It was reassuring to feel the throbbing life of the bike between my knees and the track through the handlebars as I thankfully made my way back out of the forward area. I oscillated between Army Signals and Group at this time, a practice followed throughout the desert campaign, for there was the greatest co-operation between the Eighth Army Signals and the newly formed Desert Air Force Ground Communications Control. My squadron was operating, once again, out of Kabrit on the Suez Canal, but we were no longer the 'white kneed sprogs' of a year ago. Yet, there was so much for us still to learn. While the front line men were killing and dying, the flying lads too were doing their thing, killing and dying too, the remainder of us supported and helped as best we could by doing our various jobs to the utmost.

As swiftly as our allies and we British had retreated—not without cost—it was now our turn to advance. Again, not without cost. The Eighth Army ultimately broke the Afrika Korps. It was the Matruh Race (as we called it) in reverse. The miles of Egyptian coastline with it's familiar names: Alamein, Tel el Eisa, Daba, Fuka, Matruh, Sidi Barrani, Sollum, and then into Cyrenaica (Libya of today), Fort Capuzzo, Tobruk, Benghazi, and El Aghelia. The towns, the villages, and map references tumbled one by one, some easily, some with difficulty, until finally Tripoli fell to our forward units on 23rd January 1943. Thirteen hundred miles in three months.

For me, it was as though I was attached to the front line by a huge elastic band; sometimes I was too close, sometimes a comfortable distance away. The last week in October and the weeks of November 1942 were hectic in the extreme. During the last days of October, I lead an advanced party of the squadron from Kabrit, on the Suez Canal, up to a landing ground designated L.G.237 in the Wadi Natrun area, situated off the Cairo/Alexandria road. Within a week, I was back at Kabrit to shepherd the main strength of the ground staff, armours, fitters, and transport etc., to L.G.237, ready to greet our Wellington bombers, which would drop in as soon as we were installed there. Once the squadron was established we would be poised to race into the Desert Blue if the break, which we all expected, should occur. As we know now, the break did occur. By the 4th November, the battle area front was very fluid and the Afrika Korps was retreating west from Egypt along the coastal road and through the Halfaya Pass etc. However, it was not a collapse, it was a stiff fighting withdrawal.

Within two weeks of the opening barrage of the El Alamein battle, I was with an advanced unit of my squadron at L.G.104—a landing ground cut out of the desert sand just south of the coast road between Daba and Fuka. I never saw such a scene of destruction: burnt, broken, twisted, blackened, often shapeless objects that were once guns, planes, and vehicles. They littered the whole area. And, of course, all the bric-a-brac of armies moving out; the rubbish, odd bits of clothing, personal items like letters, discarded helmets, ammo boxes, and hundreds upon hundreds of our flimsy petrol tins. L.G.104 was about 10 miles west of the old L.G.106, which had been our first desert airfield and home near Tel el Eisa. Already it seemed a lifetime since we had 'lost' our old mobile crane and driver somewhere around here.

Within a few days of the squadron being installed on L.G 104, orders came through that our bombers would be flying to Malta for an unspecified series of operations. The strategic position afforded to Malta was a constant concern to the German High Command. The supply route for the Afrika Korps across the Mediterranean was continually under threat from the RAF and Naval units operating from the island. All the Tunisian and Libyan ports available to Rommel were within easy reach of the Malta based Wellingtons. The ground personnel and all the paraphernalia associated with a bomber squadron were quickly made ready for yet another move. Once the selected Wellingtons due to go to Malta were cleared, we went back to L.G.237 on the Delta, lock, stock, and barrel. The surplus aircraft followed down once the camp there was re-installed. Various members of the ground staff were seconded to other units but the main core of the squadron staff stayed ready for the return of the bulk of our aircraft. They continued to put up some aircraft, in association with other squadrons.

After a while, I was directed to Ground Communications Control and before I realised it, I had to go nearly seven hundred miles westward to the Forward G.C.C. at Benghazi. Benghazi had just fallen, so with the barest necessities that I could carry in a standard haversack, I was off and according to common practice, as a D.R., I could 'beg' food and fuel from any unit, anywhere along my route. So north from L.G.237 to the coast road, then west along that single tar-mac road which runs for hundreds of miles with hardly a junction. For tens of miles, the road was littered with the blackened wrecks of burnt out vehicles. Sometimes there was evidence of whole clusters of trucks being caught together, tangible results of fighter-bomber attacks. Before you reach the plateau out of Egypt into Libya, there is a place called Buq Buq, which has to be the dustiest spot in the world. For about 12 miles either side of the staging post of Buq Buq, the peculiarity of the sand there is that under a crisp crust it is like talcum powder. The tar-mac of the road in that area had been severely damaged by the war traffic it had carried. Drivers had endeavoured to avoid the potholes and the terribly bad broken edges, in spite of temporary repairs, and had moved off the road but parallel to it. Each intrepid driver had moved wider and wider away from the road to avoid the choking dust from the vehicle in front but some had unfortunately found a mine with disastrous results. But no matter where you went, you ended up a very dusty and a very thirsty grey man, only to find that the staging post at Buq Buq served tea made with desalinated salt water or at worst, I suspect, filtered seawater. Up through Halfaya Pass (nick named Hell Fire by some), a long torturous route for laden lorries to the top of the plateau, there was a huge shell laying proud on the sand. I never discovered anything about it but in my ignorance - then as now - I would say it was a 16" naval shell; it was certainly the largest I've ever seen. It became a landmark. Once through the old wire—the pre-war border between Egypt and Cyrenaica—the old Italian strong point Fort Capuzzo comes into view. A hundred miles further on to Tobruk is the small port but one of major importance to the warring armies.

An Aside

Historical notes re Tobruk and the Axis Bypass.

In 1940, the Italians advanced into Egypt as far as Sidi Barrani.

In December 1940 the 'Army of the Nile' under General Wavell drove the Italian Army clear westwards; as far as El Aghelia by February 1941.

Then Rommel and his newly formed Afrika Korps re-took Cyrenaica during

---

March 1941 driving the British forces back to the Egyptian frontier. However, a garrison of Australian troops held on to Tobruk behind the enemy lines and it was at this time that Rommel caused the Axis Bypass to be constructed.

Tobruk was relieved in November 1941 by the renamed Eighth Army.

The Eighth Army reached El Aghelia, yet again, in January 1942 only to suffer another offensive and reverse by the Axis powers. The British stabilised the line at a place called Gazala before continuing the withdrawal back (loosing Tobruk this time) to a semi-prepared area around El Alamein.

On 23rd October 1942, the opening barrage heralded the offensive of the Eighth Army and the Desert Air Force. This ultimately culminated in the total defeat of the Axis Partnership in North Africa, in conjunction with the First Army on the Cap Bon Peninsula.

So around Tobruk on the Axis Bypass and along the coast road is the fertile coastal area of Dernia, once occupied and tilled by Italian colonialists. Another 200 miles on to Benghazi, another shell of a town. The usual plethora of the tide of war was visible even from the thin thread of metallic road hugging the coastline. The burnt and blackened skeletons of vehicles, the little clusters of pathetic handmade crosses and haphazard graves, an occasional scrape trench and thousands upon thousands of square British petrol tins which littered the whole area.

When I got to Benghazi, I found my Forward Ground Communications Control housed in a very battered, partially roofed building and was given my pitch by a Signals Sergeant. I sorely missed my metal bed but that was a thousand miles east with John at my old squadron. However, for the short time I was based at Benghazi, I got quite comfortable. Our various front line units were in a blurred, overlapping, patchwork quilt pattern, and some 30 to 60 miles away when I first arrived in Benghazi. Other army probes were 200 miles south and there were odd troop concentrations in between. Along the coast road, there was a jumble of all kinds of vehicles jostling about, mostly moving westwards. There were about a dozen despatch riders at the F.G.C.C., two of us were Desert Air Force personnel, the rest were Army Signals but there was no discrimination amongst us. Often the major problem was locating the unit required, a map reference without adequate local knowledge, be it about mined areas outside the tapes, the confusing criss-crossing tracks and the ever present threat of trigger happy friends made the first few days fraught with danger.

The order of the day-to-day business was quickly established. At the Signals Centre we had a theoretical ten hours on duty and ten on stand down but in practice it was more of a case of 'if you are in, then out  you go'. The local terrain became very familiar although the location of the various units, and the units themselves, were changing from hour to hour.

Quite suddenly it would rain. It was always a downpour. Within minutes, the countryside would be a quagmire. The wadis, which are no more than natures' canals switching across the undulating ground, fulfilled their purpose and became rushing, uncrossable torrents in minutes. To be wet and exposed to unseen dangers was bad enough but when the daylight fell, it got very cold as well. Even without the rain, nights felt cold after the warmth of the day.

Every day the war line moved forward, mainly in leaps and bounds. Sometimes, it would only be a mile or two if the enemy decided to slow us up. Another time, the jump would be 30 to 50 miles or more. Within a week or so, the F.G.C.C. moved forward and six of us moved even further forward, to the advanced F.G.C.C. echelon. In less than three hours there, we had lost two D.R.'s, one by a mine on a side track and the other by shell splinters. For several weeks the work was hard and extremely dangerous but it became progressively less so as the confronting army groups moved inextricably away to the west.

Never-the-less, the war had been very close to me and my boyish enthusiasm for war and the excitement it all generated had started to wane. To struggle forward, often in the open, to units whose main objective, unless ordered otherwise, was to keep their heads down demanded the utmost from me that I was capable of at that time. However, I would not have changed places with any of the army guys even though they would probably be out of the line in about nine days. Never-the-less, early December and the war front - although it was hardly a front more like a honeycomb of strongly held areas - was relatively quiet. I quickly learnt the position of every burnt and wrecked vehicle out in the blue, the mined areas, the little groups of crosses and the various piles of personal junk, the discarded odds and ends of military hardware and, of course, every wadi and track of that north-western corner of Cyrenacia. By the second week of December the Axis had evacuated El Aghelia due to the constant pressure of the Eighth Army, the Desert Air Force and, of course, the coastal harassment by the Royal Navy. We had now turned the corner of the Gulf of Sirte and on our way to Tripoli.

El Aghelia was a tremendous milestone  for us in the desert; we were all braking new ground now. Aghelia had been an obstacle twice before but now it was ours and we felt like winners. A few miles down the road to the old border between Cyrenacia and Tripolitania Mussolini had built a huge monumental gateway over the road, which we called the Marble Arch. It commemorated his military acquisition of Cyrenaica in the 1930's. I passed through it sometime before Christmas Day (I know now that it was taken on Dec 15th) but I have no recollection of Christmas Day or of the Christmas Season 1942, but I do remember seeing 1943 in. On my way back to Signals HQ, I found myself short of petrol so I called into an encampment for some. D.R.'s were always welcome as carriers of the latest "gen," be it rumour or real news of what was happening elsewhere. I was cordially invited to the mess tent where, and when, I realised it was New Years Eve. I stayed and joyfully saw the New Year in with the gunners and their 'free' drinks and rations.

Very replete I slept soundly. When I got back to my HQ late in the afternoon of the following day, I was disconcerted to discover that I had been posted adrift overnight and was listed as 'missing'. I can't recall the story I told to cover my indiscretion but I am sure I felt it was worth it.

I was twenty years of age.

One day I had to go an area we called "The Tripoli Box" - it was an area like a bulge poking into ground overlooked by the Axis troops - on a routine matter, when I was grabbed by a very senior Intelligence Officer and taken to the Commanding Officer on the site. I was instructed, in precise terms, to take a special small package to a specific map reference and hand it to the aide of a named Air Chief Marshal and on no account to part with it to anyone below a

Group Cartain (a Colonel). This was big stuff and rated Top Priority. Two Arm Bands, no less, for a DR carrying such a package! Off I went feeling very special and glad to have the excuse to get out of the 'box' and away from the odd shell that seemed to have my name on it. I speedily got out and on to the coast road and headed for the rear. Checking my map, I turned off down a well defined track until I saw ahead a large marquee and some trailers. As I got closer, I noticed two distinguished looking officers standing outside and feeling my position as a very special D.R. I swept onto the site in the grand manner followed by an enormous cloud of dust that covered all and sundry. As the cloud drifted away, I dismounted, I then saluted as smartly as I could and asked for the aide of the Air Marshall. The smaller man held out his hand and then I saw the insignia; he was the Air Marshall! Afterwards I wondered about the IQ of VIP's; an ordinary airman would have, at least, turned his back to the dust cloud. Or were they were so deep in conversation they never saw or heard me coming? I never discussed it with them but made my escape faster than I had arrived.

Events were coming to a conclusion in this part of Tripolitainia and Tripoli was captured on the 23 January 1943 and I found myself in the town the end of that month, trying to settle in at yet another location, although the accommodation this time was a large Italian colonial house complete with a roof. But early in February, I was relieved to get orders to go back to my squadron, which was still at L.G.237, some 1300 to 1500 miles to the east. I assumed that our aircraft on secondment to Malta were returning and that proved to be the case.

I had reservations about my bike making it back to the Delta so here and now might be a good time to make a few observations about motorbikes and riding them in desert war-time conditions; and maybe some general comments on transport in the Western Desert. Tyres, particularly for motorbikes, were always a huge problem. Even if you were meticulous in your attention to tyre pressures, removing flints etc., they hardly ever had more than 750 miles of track running in them. At best, having a mixture of tarmac and track running, a change was always necessary between 3000 and 5000 miles. And lorry tyres hardly fared any better. Sand dust was a constant problem too. It rapidly joined forces with the grease that was essential for the obvious moving parts like brake and clutch levers, drive chains, steering forks and the steering itself. Sand dust and grease became a very efficient grinding paste, and before long, every part was a very sloppy fit! Air filters were also a joke; they clogged up so quickly that the temptation was great to remove them altogether but that opened up the whole of the engine to the ever present sand dust. Mixed with the oil it became a different kind of grinding medium but it worked equally well and it wasn't long before one could rattle the piston inside of the pot (cylinder) Loss of performance and a blue haze as one battered along indicated oil was being burnt due to the sloppy piston rings. The unmentionable oil filters need not be mentioned. Sand and dust would quickly find it's way into the petrol tank from a variety of sources but the result was always the same; blocked fuel lines.

Desert sores were not the prerogative of DR's but by the very nature of riding a motorbike, in the desert environment, aggravated any poor skin condition. The unremitting rubbing of sand-choked linen and cotton on sun or wind-burnt skin could become very painful. I didn't suffer a great deal from desert sores and my only main example of the condition I have already documented. The only other skin problem I really experienced with motorbikes was jumping, without thinking, onto the bike which had stood in the sun and having the inside of my bare thighs stick to the red hot petrol tank leaving skin behind. Very painful indeed; and a ready made wound for a 'desert patch' rather than a sore! My friend John organised a petrol tank cover for me. It once graced the back of a chair in the Kursaal restaurant in Cairo. Talking of 'red hot petrol tanks' reminds me that petrol evaporated away from the tank vent nearly as quick as the engine consumed it. A bike standing in the sun could loose practically all it's petrol in half a day. In a khamsin wind, (a very hot wind blowing mainly in March) the petrol going into the carburettor could evaporate away before reaching the engine and the bike would just peter out. Happened often to lorries too. One would always be careful of opening a tin that had stood in the sun, be it water or petrol. They could be under such pressure that they would literally explode when the cap was released. A badly scalded face, or wherever, was treated as a 'self inflicted injury'.

So as I said, 1500 miles or so to L.G.237 on the Delta. Wherever I stopped on the long haul back I was milked of every scrap of information by the news hungry fellows on what was happening up front. Finally back on my squadron again and into a different world from the F.G.C.C.

John was very pleased to see me again, almost as though I'd come back from the dead. I reclaimed my bed, but he was still glad to have me back, he said! Flossie—remember the little dog of Kabrit?—had had some pups, and John had kept one for himself that he called Barbara for some reason. While I can say that Flossie made a great show of recognising me, it was obvious that she had now become the Cookhouse Dog and who can blame her.

Barbara, the pup, was utterly devoted to John and never seemed to leave his side. The rest of Flossie's litter were distributed throughout the squadron and, in time, I got to know them all, one by one. There was a great deal of anticipation and activity on the camp as our Wellington aircraft had arrived back from Malta only the day before I had. The fellows who had been temporarily sent to other outfits, like me, were finding their way back too. The squadron had acquired a few new trucks, and with a new crane, they made our total transport count in excess of fifty units. I also got a new bike from the Transport Pool at Heliopolis. This was the third or fourth since I had arrived in the Middle East. I recollect it was one of my favourites; the first of several of this type that I was to be issued with. It was a 350cc Matchless with the new 'telescopic' front forks instead of the old open link forks with their sand and grease problems.

So the preparations were well in hand for the big move. We were going to head for Soluch. This was the airfield area way south of Benghazi towards El Aghelia.

Familiar ground for me but fresh for the squadron and a long way away. At last, the camp was struck and the whole squadron was on the move, fifty-odd vehicles filled with men and material plus the new mobile crane and our old ambulance followed by the fitter's wagon. The so-called 'fitters wagon' carried all the spares for the motor transport, including a bundle of tyres and, of course, my bed. This whole column was spearheaded by the Despatch Rider with the Convoy Commander (the Transport Warrant Officer) following in an old service car. The field kitchen of three vehicles was half an hour ahead of the main body. I was the D.R., and the general routine was to go forward about ten miles, check the ground forward and/or leaguer points then count the trucks as they safely passed by me, and open up the gaps between the vehicles if they were bunching (ideally 80 to 100 yards apart), I reported often to the Convoy Commander and fussed over the convoy as though they were chicks. John, the co-driver of the fitter's wagon, was theoretically always the last truck. If any of the convoy broke down on the roadside then the fitters would do whatever was necessary to get them going again; and I would be two vehicles missing as I counted them through. The large wheel jack carried by the fitters eased the chore of wheel changing, one of the major problems encountered by a convoy run. There were always a number of possible sites to leaguer overnight, pre-planned by the Convoy Commander and the nearest to the required time to stop or refuel. Food was basic and sleeping was rough for everyone. There were no luxuries like washing or shaving and not much in the way of a prepared breakfast, so it was always an early start with few things to cause any delay.

As we neared it, Buq Buq lived up to its reputation. The sand dust made driving impossible for the following vehicle causing each driver to edge out in echelon. My convoy of fifty lorries ended up over at least four miles in three great swages each about a thousand yards wide. I ended up looking like a plaster cast. The fourth day on the road and things were going fine; then I realised that I'd 'lost' the ambulance. John, with the fitter's wagon, hadn't seen it, so it was a problem. While the convoy went on to a prearranged map reference, I went back some twenty miles without any sign of the ambulance. I then retraced my steps again, this time to rejoin the main body, guessing that, for some unknown reason, the ambulance had left the road. I was going to get some food and then do another search, but before I got to the leaguer, it began to get windy and the lighter dust lifted readily and began to swirl. By the time the daylight closed down, there was a full-scale dust storm blowing. The sand screened the road and it became difficult to say where the road ended and the sand edge began, and it took no time at all for the road to be completely indistinguishable. I bumped along going slower and slower into the gritty wind when, suddenly, right in front of me were strands of wire. I propped my bike against a wire post and I slowly felt my way along the wire looking for a gap but found a notice instead. My fears were realised, the word *Minen* under the usual skull and cross bones, except that I was on the wrong side! I slowly followed the wire back to my bike and huddled down as best I could, for a very long, chilly, and uncomfortable night.

 At first light, I quickly found the road again and discovered that I had ridden some two miles through the minefield. I subsequently found the ambulance in a wadi with a flat tyre. The driver wasn't popular with me, the Convoy Commander or John. Rather stiff, very dirty, and extremely tired, I had the cooks hash me something up for the road. I remember that the bunks in the ambulance looked very inviting! My convoy, evenly spaced out like beads on a string, swept majestically around the promontory of northern Cyrenaica. We were not fearful of enemy air attacks here even though, as I have said, there was enough debris about to prove to anyone that the tide of war had passed this way.

Eventually we turned south down towards our new airfield at Soluch. The earth is a reddish colour, somewhat similar to Devonian soil but that is where the similarity ceases. It is covered with a sparse, spiky grass with an occasional desert shrub plant of some sort or another, which flowers in February. This was such a change from the naked stony sand and the odd desert thorn so prevalent over hundreds of square miles up until now. Once we arrived on site, the Transport Planning Officer directed specific groups to their designated areas: cooks and mess tents, Intelligence and Photographic trailers, the armours, the motor transport, here, there and wherever.

After a couple of days of hectic activity to become an operational squadron, orders came through for us to move on again. For me, it was quite hard to come to terms with the fact that it was such a short time ago that this 'field' was virtually our very advanced Forward Ground Communications Control echelon, later to become a fighter station. The fact that it was now considered to be too far from the front line for a Wellington Bomber Squadron gives some idea of the pace of the Eighth Army's advance.

We were now destined to go to Gardabia, about 15 or 18 miles from the coast at Misurata; at least another

400 miles west. The front line, a further 200 miles west of our proposed new location, was where the Eighth Army was closing down onto the Mareth Line area. Rommel was hoping to stabilise his Afrika Korps there on prepared defences. The battle zone would be just over an hours flying time from Gardabia, saving at least four or five hours on a round trip from Soluch. So all through the routine of breaking camp again, the loading of the lorries and all the arrangements that have to be made when a unit moves. In due time, we were all off again. Near the old border of Cyrenaica and Tripolitania, I ushered my convoy through Mussolini's Marble Arch. The solitary white structure, standing astride the narrow black tarmac road in the shimmering air, was a new sight for our travelling ground staff. The convoy trundled on until we left

the metallic coast road near Misurata and headed inland on one of the most rutted and god-awful tracks that I could have possibly lead a convoy on. The 15 miles or so took best part of a day. Many of the lorries were bogged down in the soft dust of the rutted track and had to be manhandled out on metal track pans pushed under wheels, which had sunk to their hubs. In some sections, there were large rocks beneath the surface, which caused the lorries to crab across the track, ever in danger of tipping them right over. Each lorry looked like a small ship in a rough storm at sea giving men and materials a very rough ride indeed. And through all this, the red dust kicked up by the activity, drifted slowly away in a great plume. We had to be grateful that the time of intense active enemy air aggression had passed. We settled in at Gardabia and, to our general surprise, the targets we started to hit were the Palermo docks and shipping around Sicily. When one looks at the whole strategic picture, it is not so surprising really but down at my level, even as a D.R. with all my snippets of information, you had a very blinkered view of the war around you.

Malta proved a God-send to one of our crews who managed to 'drop in' there one night on the way back with some trouble. Without the 'stop over' island of Malta, it would have been a crew and an aircraft lost in the drink! But before long, we were attacking Axis airfields just behind the Mareth Line, which we took as a good sign that the Eighth would be moving against the German line soon. Quite suddenly, the weather deteriorated and it was very cold and windy. Then it rained, operations were cancelled and I have recollections of quagmire and of a number of fellows being washed out of their tents because they had pitched them in shallow gullies out of any wind but right in the path of rushing water that had nowhere else to go! We had a number of operations on Palermo, with Messina as an alternative, before we went back to the Mareth battle area.

I was doing the things that D.R.s do in static situations. I was carrying despatches between squadron, wing and group Intelligence Officers and when not required to be 'at the ready' I would spend my, not inconsiderable, spare time

scrounging around the area, sometimes with John and sometimes not, taking pictures which were processed, in the main, by the photographers. Later these pictures were sold to the squadron chaps at a huge profit.

Sometimes at night, while I waited for the return of the aircraft, I would join the photographers in the trailer processing pictures and drinking local wine. There is a chemical called Potassium Permanganate sometimes used in photography for staining night picture negatives. It is a strong red colour in solution, and apart from its photographic use, it is also good for curing athlete's foot. We used to keep our private wine in a cupboard in the photographic trailer but one of the chaps (Sid Inward's name comes to mind) felt sure that some-else was drinking his wine when he wasn't there. So, he secretly rinsed out a demi-john and poured his red wine into it labelling it Permanganate. On a change of night shift, someone—we never found out who—had need of some Permanganate. Finding it didn't work, he made a new batch, substituting it for the wine. When eventually Sid had time to swig his demi-john, a fair swallow had gone down his gullet before he could stop. His language was disgusting.

The day to day routine was uneventful; the war seemed a long way away. It wasn't really but we were not being subjected to any direct enemy action and the various aircrews that we lost from time to time did not really hurt, unless you had made personal friends of them. Very often one would say something like "Fancy losing R for Robert last night," a reference to the aircraft rather than the crew. We didn't only lose them over the target area either. One night we had a plane come back with some bombs 'hung-up'. The crew had tried to dislodge them while in the air, but on landing, they had come down blowing the aircraft to smithereens. All the crew were killed except for the rear gunner who miraculously escaped with a broken leg and burns. Rear gunners were often 'lucky' when it came to a crash and there are many cases recorded of the "tail-end Charlie" being thrown clear.

The Eighth Army was doing great but on our little patch we were having a bad time. Our losses in April were quite heavy; we even had one of our Wellingtons not lifting on take-off and exploding at the end of the runway. There was an obvious strain on lots of the people intimately involved in the squadron's activities but the days went on. It was about now when our losses were at the worst for a long time that there was an accident on a sister squadron. We shared our runway, which was scraped out of the brown earth and scrub, with a Halifax Squadron, huge four engine aeroplanes (our Wellingtons had two). One morning there was a hell of a thump. There had been a Halifax bomber standing over two trolleys of bombs and the whole lot had gone up. There was just black smoke and flaming wreckage. There were some survivors from among the armours working there but heaven knows how. While the rescuers were racing over to the plane there were further sharp cracks and thumps as more of the bomb load went up. Bits of metal were flying about and some ended up half a mile from the scene. There were at least a dozen killed and there were gory stories of bits of human limbs being picked up. The next time I went into Misurata, I was asked about the huge bang and oily smoke; they had heard it and seen the plume of black smoke some fifteen miles away.

One day I experienced a very bizarre event, one that no-one could possibly have imagined. Even I refused to believe it at first. I had just made a despatch drop to our Group Intelligence tent and as I rode back, a snake raised its head in the gap between the steering and the petrol tank. With my hands locked on the steering bars, I couldn't seem to get my face far enough away from the snake's head as it weaved about. Faster than I can say, I stopped and yanked the bike onto it's stand, the engine still ticking over. I remember standing back surveying the bike and wondering what to do. A remark to a couple of passing airman that I had a snake in my bike didn't generate the sort of response that I'd hoped for. The snake was nowhere to be seen, but I surely wasn't going to get on the bike again before I knew where it had gone. Eventually the problem sorted itself out because the engine had become very hot and the vibration had the rear wheel spinning freely. The unfortunate reptile vacated the area over the hot engine and slithered down and got caught up in the driving chain and died. It was an adder of course. As I rode away, and for many days afterwards, I kept looking down expecting another snake.

It was khamsin type weather by early May, terribly hot and dry. The hot wind feels as though it's from an oven and there's nowhere to hide from it. Even moving through the air on a motorbike gives little respite from it, and every now and again, the wind is strong enough to raise the dust, driving choking dust into wildly flapping tents.

One hot and lazy afternoon on the airstrip at Gardabia and we were idly watching the approach of one of our

WELLINGTON BOMBER

Two Hercules engines 1370 HP each
Crew five Pilot, Navigator/Bomb Aimer, Radio Op.
Gunners.

Wing Span 86 feet. Length 64 feet 7 inches.
Bomb Load 5,100 lbs.

Wellingtons. It seemed to be coming in just a shade too fast and a little too high. As we watched, the nose dropped sharply and only at the last moment did the nose lift but not quite enough to stop the plane from ploughing in heavily as the undercarriage legs collapsed. The aircraft skidded and slew about in a huge cloud of dust for hundreds of yards amid the noise of roaring engines and tearing metal, bent props and bits of debris flying everywhere. Everyone started to run but I got there first on my motorbike. F/Lt Langton - the pilot - was dazed and had a horrifying gash half way round his scalp with blood pouring forth but we got him out - the navigator and I - through the astrodome and we hobbled away like a couple in a three legged race. We were a hundred yards or so from the plane (always a chance that the thing would burst into flames with so much fuel leaking out) before the first of the running ground staff or the crash wagon reached us. A week later Langton, full of smiles, returned to the squadron with his head and nose all bandaged up. He took me into the Officers Mess (with the C.O.'s sanction) for a drink.

An Aside

Over twenty years later, in my civilian job as an Industrial Staff Photographer for a nationally known dairy company, I attended the commissioning of a new yoghurt plant at Wootton Bassett, Wiltshire. The opening ceremony was to be conducted by the Chairman of the Wiltshire County Council, one Sir Henry Langton. We recognised each other immediately. Unfortunately, the national press photographers and reporters felt that the meeting of Sir Henry Langton and the desert "hero" was a much better story than yoghurt, much to my embarrassment and the chagrin of my directors.

The Eighth Army had successfully pushed through the fortifications of the  German Mareth Line, while a New Zealand contingent threatened to out-flank the defences. Our bombers had continued to tackle targets in the battle zone, as well as visiting the Sicilian ports on a regular basis. During April, Sfax fell followed by Sousse and Kairouan. The First Army finally took Tunis and Bizerta at the end of the first week in May and, although there was still some fierce fighting by fanatical Nazi units in the Envidaville, Zaghuon, Kairouan triangle, the war was virtually over, but it was not until the 12th May 1943 that the North African Campaign was officially declared over.

I MUST FINISH this section with a sad little story that started (and ended) here in May yet started, and ended with me a month from now. I received a letter, sometime in June, expressing sorrow that my cousin Dennis had been killed in North Africa. Dennis, three years my senior, was a member of the pre-war amateur British Territorial Army. At the outbreak of war in 1939, he went to France with the first contingent. As a young N.C.O., he was taken off the beaches at Dunkirk. The next time that I knew of his whereabouts, he was in Iraq with the 56th(London) Division. By June, as this narrative will show, I was in Kariouan and the only place Dennis could have been killed was here. If Dennis had been killed here abouts, then the local Graves Registration Unit would have him listed. Sure enough, although they had misspelled his name, which I corrected, there he was.

D. Fenning. Company Sergeant Major. 56 (London) Division

General Sir William Jackson in The North African Campaign 1940-43 says of this time:

"Eighth Army made one more effort on 28th April using the newly arrived and inexperienced 56th (London) Division which had motored from Iraq to Envidaville, some 3,200 miles, in 32 days. It seized its objectives, but was thrown into disorder by counter-attacks."

The Graves Unit gave me a map reference

and, eventually, I headed towards a group of very small trees or saplings in the flat landscape. Through the white taped lines, I slowly rode my bike, one foot on the ground along by a rail track. Over a small wadi the rail was carried by a low level sideless little trestle bridge and, as I got nearer, the saplings turned out to be a staggered little group of up turned rifles, stuck, bayonet down, into the ground, with a little cross here and there. There were six or eight graves in this lonely spot somewhere near Envidaville. The whole area was heavily mined and I had to walk very gingerly inside a narrow channel formed by usual white tapes. I photographed the graves and sent the pictures back home.

Dennis had been killed by mortar fire on the 11th May. Such a tragic thing, only hours before the official cease fire of May 12th.

I visited the area several times and re-photographed the site. Much later, on comparing the various pictures, I noticed that there had been a cap badge nailed to the wooden cross; it was missing on the later versions.

What a pity I did not think to take it.

I have often wondered who did, but I hope it was a friend.

CHAPTER NINE

VICTORY IN AFRICA

THE EUPHORIA THAT THE WAR was over lasted for two whole days, then we learnt that we were to become part of the North West African Strategic Air Force (BNAF or British North African Force - to us) commanded overall by a famous American, Major-General James Doolittle USAAF.

We were to loose our Desert Air Force tag and, I suppose, in consequence of the change of command and our place in the overall bombing plan, we were to move

500 odd miles west to Kairouan in Tunisia. In the few days before we actually moved, John & I spent a day in Leptus Magna. This is an ancient Roman city close to the modern Libyan town of Homs. The ruins of the Forum and theatre were excavated by Italian scholars, and a marvellous job they had made of it. It is a magnificent site (no pun intended) and not only did I photograph everything for the sets of pictures we would sell to all our ground-crew later, but John and I took turns at photographing each other sitting on the enormous stone thrones that were scattered among the fallen pillars and columns.

The visit was worth the run in spite of the awful track to and from the main road. Before we left, I scouted out and found an alternative route for our convoy and, in due course, off we went. It was just another convoy except that, en route, we 'lost' a man. The dusty trucks, full of our wide-eyed ground staff, bowled through Tripoli. I noticed a great change in the demeanour of the local inhabitants and a general clean up of rubbish and debris.

We kept going - not counting short stops. Eventually we leagued overnight in an Italian colonial plantation with fig and other trees. I never had a chance to speak to him but apparently one of our lads climbed onto a lorry cab to reach into a tree. Whether it was a fig he was after or something else but a booby trap exploded taking his hand off and shattering his arm. He was immediately treated by our doctor, and later he was taken by ambulance to the local medical unit. We heard later that he had lost an eye as well; he never returned to our unit of course.

The Mareth Line seemed a disappointment to me at first, considering that I expected obvious fortifications; never-the-less, as one progressed through the Wadi Akarit area there were the pathetic graves and cairns of stones on each side of the road and mines - thousands upon thousands of them - black triangles, skull and cross bone signs saying "Minen." The infamous Wadi Akarit is very deep and straight sided, a very miniature Grand Canyon and the road took a devious route down, up and over because all bridges were down.

At last Kariouan Cheria field and, in a few days, we were operational. Then, what a surprise, the port of Sousse, some thirty miles away, was attacked three nights running by German aircraft. The war wasn't over after all. We did not really get settled in because, in less than six weeks at Kariouan Cheria, we moved the whole squadron to a more suitable field, one less susceptible to floods. Hani West was about three miles from the Holy City of Kariouan, the 'City of a Thousand Mosques' - and a million smells - a city second only to Mecca in the Islamic Faith. We had been at Hani West barely a week when we had an alert that enemy paratroops had been dropped in the area. Everyone said it was a crack German unit who had dropped to sabotage our aircraft

but that was as far as it went. At least, it had quickened us up a bit.

There wasn't very much for me to do when the

squadrons settled down. I might rush the odd despatch or night photograph from one Intelligence Officer to another, from Squadron to Wing or Group, but it didn't amount to more than one hour in twenty-four. I'd join John or John would join me doing whatever was interesting to do. We would go to Sousse to swim but the thirty miles to the coast was a drawback.

I would also spend lots of time with the photographic people and often helped in processing. I also assisted in fitting cameras on aircraft and checking the various components necessary for night photography.

Three photographers & one D.R. Kiwi (Segt) Pop Degg, me, Sid Inwards.

There is a timing control box, called a Type 35, which is activated by the bomb aimer prior to releasing his bombs. Over the target, when the bombs are released, at the correct time interval, a four foot magnesium flash is dropped from a shute situated near the tail. Once the aircraft was bombed-up and fully loaded with its petrol requirement, the photographers would do their testing before the aircraft was signed off for 'ops'. It took two to do the last minute check of the Type 35 and the camera. One would, with some difficulty, go down the length of the Wellington aircraft, stretching awkwardly over the main spar then carefully stepping down the catwalk to the flash shute. Miss the catwalk and your foot could go through the fabric. The flash shute is a square tube standing about three feet high or so on the port side. Already in the shute would be the million candlepower magnesium flash, held up by a mechanical catch. The man at the tail would lift up the flash, slightly taking the weight, while the man up the front checked the 35 control, the sequence that operated the mechanical catch to drop the flash. On this occasion it was my turn to struggle down to the back of the aircraft while my friend, Jock Crawford, checked the 35. How the misunderstanding arose, I cannot imagine but, before I could reach the flash tube, I heard the latch click and saw the flash disappear down the tube.

For one thousandth of a second I stood still, anticipating the awful bang. I came to as I crashed my shin on the main spar, tumbling, head first, to the small exit by the pilots seat. Crawford's head was disappearing through the hole because, instinctively, he knew something was wrong and he wasn't waiting around to find out what. Jock was 200 yards from the plane before he stopped. I was beside him. We waited ages before we slowly, and very carefully, walked back, and there, balancing upright in the sand was the million candle power flash, with its release cord still attached. Had the flash not stood up in the soft sand but had fallen over, thereby pulling the vane cover free, it would have been just a matter of time before the breeze would have put enough turns on the vane for the flash to go up. That would have completely taken the tail off and there's no doubt that an almighty explosion would have followed with all those bombs and petrol on board. The armours later re-loaded the flash for us. We were not quite so blasé about things for a considerable time afterwards recalling the Halifax incident at Gardabia. The

Wing Armament Officer had considered that that had probably been due to human error in the fitting of a delayed action fuse.

The days went by and I did the normal things. I saw John often, played with Barbara the dog, boiled my washing in an petrol tin on a fire made by scooping a hole in the sand and soaking the hole with  - yes - petrol, shared cigarettes and wine with John.

Obviously even good friends fall out sometimes and one day some horse-play between John and I got out of hand. I pushed John back onto his wooden bed, which broke under his weight. He reacted immediately and a real tough slogging fight erupted between us. It went on for some time, then we became aware that the whole of the inside of the tent had blood splattered everywhere. We were both solicitous of each other, uneasy that we had seriously hurt the other. But it was me, blood was dripping from my elbow as I raised my arm to look. It was a badly cut wrist that I had sustained from his shaving mirror, which we had broken during our struggle. I still have the scar. Barbara was still barking as John bound my wrist. John and I got drunk together that night, and Barbara slept soundly.

The squadron was at full stretch, bombing targets on Sicily and on the Italian mainland. The island of Pantellaria was singled out for special treatment and after its surrender, the squadrons attention turned to Salerno, Palermo and similar targets.

The days were long and hot, with occasional heavy rain, whereas the nights were usually quite cold. Sometimes there would be a stiff wind, which would raise plenty of dust and small particles of grit like sand. There was always the insects, myriads of them, both winged and crawling. How I hated them.

Quite unexpectedly, I was instructed to report to Tunis, where I discovered that I was to be included in a regular D.R. team to carry despatches to Cairo from Tunis via a number of stations. So once again, I was to travel over all that familiar ground. I was re-equipped with a huge 750cc Harley Davidson motorbike. An obvious but doubtful bonus from the First Army's supply depot. So that was it, 250 to 300 miles a day, with a couple of legs well in excess of 300 miles. What a struggle it was to maintain. There was about a three day rest before the turn round and going all the way back. From the starting base in Tunis, one D.R. left every day so there were about six or seven stretching along the North African coast at any given time. I did it eastwards then westwards, twice, before I was returned to my squadron. They then developed the Tunis/Cairo/Tunis run into a 'pony express' system by splitting the journey up into sections. Riders would cover their section, rest, then return to their base, handing on their documents to the next D.R. We, the original riders had inaugurated a service but we had experienced several major problems which resulted in bunching up and long gaps between riders due to different skills and speeds of individual D.R.'s, the specific weather at different points along the route and, of course, mechanical failure, due to the vast overall distance. We were glad we were not expected to carry on doing the whole run in one go against a timetable.

Back to my squadron. Hani West was a good 'station' yet I half expected that we would all be on the move again, but the days went by with no suggestion of a change of venue. Sometime about now we had one of our ground crew killed and another badly injured by a lorry. They had been into Kariouan, drinking some of the illicit wine in the back streets, and were ploughed down in the darkness by a lorry, presumably a British one, as they followed the road back to camp. During these months, we were loosing aircrew and planes over the Italian night skies, in large numbers, to anti-aircraft guns, to night fighters and to pure misfortune but our perspective was so warped that we almost disregarded that compared with the concern we felt for the drunken men on the road.

Hani West was a flat sand pan with a slightly raised rim. One very hot afternoon the black Wellington bombers were shimmering in the heat haze as little figures moved about them, doing all the things that have to be done to aeroplanes to make them ready for operations. On the far perimeter Harry Collins, our petrol bowser driver, was near one of the Wellingtons getting ready to fuel it from the petrol trailer, which was pulled by the petrol bowser. Both were full of petrol. All eyes were attracted to the middle distance of the dispersal area by a 'whommp' and we could see that the petrol trailer was alight. To all of us watching, there was no doubt that the bomber was going to 'go up'. We watched in amazement as the flaming petrol trailer, belching black smoke, was pulled by the petrol bowser away from the Wellington. A short distance away the tandem stopped, and we saw the figure of Harry disappearing under it all to unhook the inferno he was pulling. He then jumped back into the main bowser and drove it away. The trailer eventually burnt itself to a crisp, but the Wellington was undamaged. Most of the squadron personnel and the C.O. had witnessed the action and Harry eventually got a medal! An M.M. I believe it was.

An Aside

Years later at the first reunion we had after the war at the Horns Oval, Kennington, Harry confided that he had never been so scared in all his life, before or since. He was sure he was going to be Court Marshalled for it and he did what he did to try to put it right. He certainly never expected to get a medal. No, he said, no-one ever asked him how it started.

I can still see him smiling mischievously over his pint of beer and it was then that I realised that he might have been smoking.

Without any preamble, the Warrant Officer in charge of transport called all the Motor Transport personnel together to tell them that a number of drivers were going to be flown down to the Delta to collect new vehicles. There was a pool of lorries at the Port of Tewfik base and forty drivers were going down to re-equip the squadrons' transport. A dozen drivers from the Suez Canal pool would join our lot to bring back the fifty-odd vehicles. Ten of our own chaps would stay with the squadron at Hani West to keep it active. I was delighted to learn that I was going down as Scout DR and John was going as driver cum fitter. A DC3 took twenty of the lads down to Kabrit, and two days later, another DC took the rest of us. The long haul was broken up into three legs or hops and it was quite a fun soaked 'reunion' at our old original station of Kabrit when we finally all got together. The station transport took our drivers down to Tewfik and I went to Ismailia to collect a new bike. It was here that, just outside the Depot gate that I slipped down into a soft dust filled shallow gully hitting a solid object very hard. Jarred and shaken, I found that I had fractured the down tube of the bike frame. Within no time at all, I was 'issued' a replacement, another Royal Enfield, by the Quartermaster in charge of stores who seemed keen to get me on my way.

I got down to Tewfik to find everything had been organised, mainly by John. New vehicles complete with Jerry petrol cans, engine oil, spare tyres and John plus all kinds of emergency rations. As we trundled along the Treaty Road, roughly following the Suez Canal to Alexandria, it was daunting to think about the distance in front of us. We had to go almost to the Mediterranean coast before turning westwards into the desert heading for Hani West in Tunisia, some 2300 miles away. They didn't expect us for at least three weeks but we had a surprise in store for them. The discipline of the drivers was good because owing to some mischance in the planning somewhere we didn't have a senior non-commission officer (NCO - Sergeant or Warrant Officer) with us. The daily mileage we covered was exceptional. A number of factors attributed to this, once we had passed the 'running in' stage of the new vehicles and, of course, the subsequent oil changes which we had to do 'on the road', as it were. The lorries being empty contributed to the lack of tyre trouble in both the inner tube and outer covers and the fact that all was new. The drivers didn't have to consider their load of equipment or the men in the back because there wasn't any. We were running virtually nose to tail because the threat of enemy air action was nil. The weather was kind as well. By general consensus, no driver would stop to brew 'char' (tea) independently and by the middle distance of the journey I had it organised that for the equivalent of the midday break I had four or five groups leagued a mile or so apart from each other. By the time we were in the Tripoli area, my squadron Transport Warrant Officer had a sensible idea of where we were via the normal radio traffic as I reported the convoy through the Provost Marshall.

We swept onto Hani West with our rather tinny hooters blaring, a full seven days earlier than was originally envisaged, with all vehicles present and correct. We thought we would surprise everyone with our early arrival and were looking forward to resting on our laurels but the tables were turned on us because, within a few hours, we were taken aback to find that our vehicles were being loaded with material. We were moving from Hani West to Oudna, a decision taken on the strength of our early appearance. At the time we didn't realise what we had done; hence a Mention in Despatches for the effort.

Oudna was a very flat area bounded, on one side, by a beautiful Roman aqueduct with its symmetrical arches stretching out into the distance. Once at Oudna, we were geared up to high-powered operations but hardly had we settled down when we were informed that we were to take a sea trip to Italy. There was some movement of the Transport personnel and I think we kept half of the Tewfik Pool drivers with us, the rest were posted away.

So once again we were on our way, this time to the Bizerta docks to await the Navy's pleasure. With a happy frame of mind, we queued up on the dock road because this seemed to mean we were going the right way, home via Italy. For two days we stayed there in that long head to tail line, while we waited for the Navy to embark us onto the L.S.T.s (Landing Ship Tank). The wait had me half expectantly scanning the sky for the Luftwaffe but it was unnecessary. Even so, what a prize we'd have made for a fighter/bomber!

Back in the United Kingdom on the 11th November '43, my father was embarking to HMT Ranchi at Gourock near Greenock in the Firth of Clyde. Exactly two years had passed since I left the very same waters for overseas service.

Under the Tunisian sun, John & I played

chess, to pass away the time as we waited in the convoy column, or walking Barbara up and down chatting to the other drivers while, at about the same time, my father was approaching the Mediterranean on his way to India. The couple or three days we spent waiting in the column was extremely uncomfortable for everyone. The lads, loaded as part of the squadron material in the backs of the lorries, obviously had no proper sleeping, feeding or toilet facilities, everything was provisional or temporary.

In due time however, shrill whistles were being blown, starter motors whirring, oily exhaust fumes drifting through the column as blue clouds and chaps running to and fro scrambling to get to their allotted vehicles.

It seemed an age before there was some movement to the dock edge where there were a dozen or more LST's moored ready for loading. After a couple of hours of deck clanking, hoarse shouting, gesticulating dock MP's, whistle blowing and the whole squadron was miraculously safely aboard. The human cargo was disgorged to the upper deck and the lorries chained and battened down. Later, when we were actually on our way out at sea, we were shocked to find that we couldn't go down to the vehicles as they were 'sealed in'; shocked because our dogs were down there without food or water. To jump ahead, I have to say that although our dogs were very distressed by the time we got to them (about four days) they were all eventually OK; I can't begin to describe how pleased they were to see us!

My father traversed the Mediterranean from Gibraltar to the Suez Canal - west to east - landing at Alexandria on 12th December '43. I left Bizerta Docks in Tunisia heading for Italy travelling roughly south to north across the Mediterranean, landing at Taranto on the 1st December '43, so our paths did actually cross although we didn't meet. It's also ironic to think that he was in Port Tewfik shortly after I was there, collecting lorries on his way to India. As I believe I have said, we were not destined to meet until after the war, and that was going to be on the desolate, end of the line, platform of Harwich.

I had no idea where my father was, but right now I was heading for Sunny Italy!

CHAPTER TEN

INTO SUNNY ITALY
(Foggia & Naples)

THE JOURNEY ACROSS THE MEDITERRANEAN sea was without incident. We sailed in stately fashion, in perfect order, with nothing untoward happening to frighten us landlubbers. A totally different story from that of the sailors who had tried to reach Malta not so very long before, or indeed, those enemies of ours, who had had to run the gauntlet of the Navy and Air Force when they had tried to relieve

Rommel, even less time ago.

On the LST's we slept on the deck and tried to keep out of the way of our navy hosts. It got colder and wetter the nearer to the toe of Italy we got. My imagined picture of Italy was not like this.

The big Navy ships screened us into Taranto harbour, and we docked under a dark, wet sky with a biting wind,  which chilled us to the bone. The first bright spot was the reunion with the dogs as the off-loading was organised. The second up-lift was the tot of rum issued to all by the Navy. I'd never had rum before, free or otherwise, but this was something very different, it tainted my metal mug for ages afterwards.

I quickly made friends with some local D.R.'s who, unofficially, kitted me out with some, badly needed, spare gear that they had. We had landed with only a desert kit and it was well over a week before we got more suitable clothing.

After full assembly just outside the dock perimeter, we headed in the freezing temperatures towards Cerignola, 100 miles or so north of Taranto.

I was miserable enough, but at least I had the benefit of the second-hand D.R. top clothes. The lads curled in the backs of the lorries however, although shielded from the cold wind, were frozen solid. Around the Cerignola field, the tents were pitched in fading light, and we got our second generous tot of rum. The following day, our Wellingtons landed on the very short runway. But in less than a week, we learnt that we were to move north to Foggia, a huge airfield complex that had been put together by a vast army of American and British earth-moving battalions. The town of Foggia and its environs was still suffering from the tide of war that had swept through, even though it had been in our hands for many weeks. Bombed out buildings, desolation, and debris everywhere, scenes to be repeated far and wide. Squalid streets with ragged women shuffling about dressed in tattered black rags, precocious children begging, stealing anything to keep alive. There were signs of the previous occupiers, German notices painted on walls partially covered with English signs proclaiming the square as Oxford Circus and a street as the Old Kent Road etc.

Outside the town, we halted the convoy on the fringe of the area destined to become our squadron patch. The Convoy Commander in his small truck, with me in support, then scouted ahead to decide where we would settle our squadron HQ. The country road selected contained a series of evenly spaced-out white faced farm houses, built by Mussolini, each with its associated piece of land. One of the families was going to be ousted without ceremony, so that the house could become the squadron office. Quite arbitrarily, it was 'this one' and, without any compassion, we physically moved the family out onto the road amid much screaming and shouting which was curbed by the waving of revolvers plus a shot or two into the air and the odd push. We still considered them enemies although, by this time, they had officially changed sides. The evacuated family were housed along the road with another family, but, at the time, we couldn't have cared less and just wanted them out. Ultimately the whole road was cleared of the Italian peasant families.

The convoy was collected and the basic planning decisions were made regarding the various locations of the motor transport personnel, the armoury, the fitters lines and, of course, the essential cookhouse marquee and cook staff. In the months ahead, very little change was made to the layout of the squadron ground staff accommodation. I found myself allocated an area on the edge of a vineyard.

The first few days at Foggia Main were hectic in the extreme but eventually the jigsaw of our new situation, the location of the Squadron, Wing and Group Intelligence tents, the foreign sounding Italian place names and the multiplicity of the local tarmac roads, all fell into place.

Everything for an operational squadron had to be brought in; bomb stocks, petrol, general ammunition, food, new supplies of clothing, everything and in the mist of it all our Wellingtons flopped in from Cerignola, barely twenty air miles away. The airfield was already occupied by a large American fighter group called Lightnings and Thunderbolts. The fighters were destined to be joined by a huge contingent of Flying Fortresses.

No one had told us that Barbara was pregnant, and amid all the rushing about, we acquired a whole new doggie family. I choose my pup by moving them from mother and putting them, in a circle, about a yard away around the primus heater in the middle of the tent. I claimed the one that got to the heater first amid the general hubbub of whimpering and cheering by the lads in Johns tent. I gave him the brilliantly original name of Bobbie!

Christmas Day 1943 was bitterly cold with flurries of snow on the wind. The war seemed a million miles away and so did England; come to think of it, Sunny Italy seemed a million miles away as well yet here we were. I never knew Southern Italy could be so cold. Foggia is situated at the head of a long plain on the eastern side of the Apennines and is the grain centre of Italy. I was to find that it gets even colder, much colder, in the mountains in January and February.

The last days of 1943 seemed to drain the skies of every drop of water. It rained and rained. Everywhere off the tarmac roads and stone paths was a sea of mud. Tents and everything in them was a sodden mess (that is an unintentional pun).

Yet, some spirits were high because the New Year of 1944 was ushered in with flashing searchlights and coloured star shells. Every gun that could be fired was fired. Bofors, heavy A.A. guns, machine guns with and without tracer, rifles, and even revolvers were pointed to the heavens and fired. By the very nature of things, shrapnel and spent bullets came down, dare I say it, like rain? It was certainly tin hat time.

The weather was extremely cold for us "Desert Rats." By the end of the first week of the New Year, it snowed. Several inches fell on the plain of Foggia, and there was several feet in many of the mountain passes.

The activity around Foggia was tremendous. Constant comings and goings of petrol bowsers and trucks full of the munitions of war, both men and material. New American fighter and bomber squadrons were coming in and making themselves 'at home' on the other side of the Foggia field. We seemed to have complete supremacy of the skies for we suffered no enemy attacks on the airfield complex and the huge tented area that was developing. That, however, belied the situation because the German fighters and ground defences took a heavy toll of our attacking bombers over the selected targets. There was stiff opposition and we were loosing planes to very aggressive fighter defence.

Over the first days, I was very busy with squadron matters. Signals, service status sheets, Intelligence reports, operational night pictures and such things were  moved about rapidly from one place to another. Our squadron, in fact the whole of the British group (our group controlled four wings which, in turn, controlled eight squadrons plus a Canadian squadron) was pressing attacks on targets in northern Italy. I was running between squadron, wing and group HQ, to Bari on the east coast and across to Naples on the west side. On the coast in the Bay of Naples is an ancient Fort and this was the nerve centre of our signal exchange network system. I was a frequent visitor there.

The American Fifth Army on the left - west coast - and the British Eighth Army on the eastern side were, by now in a stalemate situation, oscillating into and out-of a set of fortifications stretching across the Italian countryside from coast to coast, later to be known as the Gustav Line.

The spine of mountains of the central Italian peninsular, as we saw them, swept from the north-east, from the peak of Monte Cairo at 5,500 feet, and Monte Baghella, 4,800 feet in the Lazio region, down to Monte Cassino. Monte Cassino at 1,700 feet stands as the last - or first - bastion of the true Apennines, crowned as it was, by its famous building, the accepted mother of all Christian monasteries, with its view of incredible majesty.

The way up to Rome on Route Six (Via Casilina) through the Liri Valley was blocked by the massif of Monte Cassino. Cassino, and its monastery, was the main pivot of the German defences; an impregnable all-seeing lookout point, the indescribable view of the lower flat plain which put fear into the Allied troops, be they American, French, Polish, Indian, Canadian, New Zealanders or British (and British includes the Irish, Welsh, Scottish and English) who crawled across the floor of the valley. Route Six actually ran through the centre of the small town of Cassino, which stood at the head of the Liri Valley which, itself, is only four to six miles wide. (The modern re-built town of Cassino is a mile west of the original town)

Somewhere up the road beyond the line, south of Rome, we learnt that there had been a coastal landing, by a combined Anglo/American force, at a place called Anzio and nearby Nettuno. We quickly just called it "Anzio" - the Antium of Antiquity and the birthplace of Nero.

It was all happening; so very much was happening. All the squadrons as well as Wings and Group now had their full strength D.R. compliment, and just when I thought it was going to be easier, four of us D.R.'s got a temporary posting. I collected a new bike. An A.J.S. and my old bike went to the Intelligence Officer who hankered after it. I also had new sparse kit issued, although John said he would look after my general gear, tent, Bobbie-the-dog and, of course, my bed. We were sent across to Bari and seconded to Army Signals. Within a few days the four of us were switched across to Naples and worked out of there for several months, mixing freely with the Americans. They used jeeps instead of bikes, but when they couldn't use jeeps, they used us. However, when they couldn't use us, they used ground runners; but there were times when it all got mixed up. We found that we often had to go beyond where we could even use a 'bike and ended up being a ground runner, greatly increasing our chances of becoming a casualty.

I had noticed an increasing number of British troops in the predominant American zone, which I attributed to the Anzio landings. I also began to carry heavy despatch bags to the New Zealand contingent.

CHAPTER ELEVEN

CASSINO

MY FIRST INTRODUCTION TO THE town of Cassino was one I could have done without. I have to admit though that at the time I had no idea that I was as close as I was to the actual town. My instructions were fairly clear and I had a good idea where the unit was that I was supposed to be going to. However, just before I reached the command post in the little village whose name escapes me now, I was viciously blown off the small road into the cold slushy mud, amid the noise and mental confusion caused by a near miss of - something! I slowly collected my thoughts. My head was thumping, and my sight was blurred. As I regained full consciousness, I realised that there was now a steady crashing of the business ends of shells and mortars falling all around the area. Keeping low, I saw that the headlamp of my bike was smashed flat as though it had been hit with a sledgehammer. Although there was still some petrol splashing about in the tank, the filler cap on top had been ripped completely out. The top of the tank looked as though it had been diagonally cleaved apart by a giant tin opener. The leg of my D.R. trousers was torn from my boot to my belt and I was covered in mud. I went back to a nearby Dressing Station hoping for some replacement trousers but the best the medics could do for me was to clean up my muddy leg and iodine my grazes. Then they gave me some safety pins for my flapping wet trousers. I got some extra petrol, which sloshed about everywhere, and I finally delivered my documents forward. Gladly I retired back to the Signals Centre.

Before long, I was once again in the same dressing station. A mortar shell had dropped killing a man for sure and wounding those who were near him, including me. I realized that I had blood dripping off each finger like milk from a cow's udder. "Bloody hell," I thought. "I've lost my left arm!" At the dressing station, a busy medic took a look, washed my arm down, and painted it with something. It turned out that a myriad of steel or stone fragments had nicked my entire arm through my thick battle blouse and at odd spots on my left leg but the medic shrugged it off telling me I'd be all right. Although badly shaken I returned again to the signals centre. To this day, I have a number of small scars, a visible reminder of those days.

It's difficult for me now to put events of the following three or four months in any chronological order; indeed, I realise now that I am finding it impossible to relate many of the events of those terrible days and nights. My remembered life over this particular time is blurred and mixed up; more like a series of clips, a patchwork of isolated incidents, mates and associates just disappearing so I will content myself with a few major events, the timings of which are well known. I can recall the early days of the war with precision, and after Cassino, I have no problems at all. But Cassino was and is so different, so very different.

There was not an exact equivalent on the Italian front of the F.G.C.C. (Forward Ground Communications Control) of the Western Desert, but there was a kind of loose collection of forward Signal Control Centres but they did work differently. However, it was from one of these that I often acted as a Ground Runner. Owing to the nature of the active front of the Gustav Line D.R.'s could use their bikes to the so-called 'Red Line', from there it was forward on foot.

The beginning of a brief, yet lifelong lasting experience for me, was when I tagged on behind a small group of soldiers moving forward one evening in the fading light. I was inside our 'Red Line' so I was on foot heading the same way as the staggered single line of Yank infantry. There was a great deal of tension in our hearts - well, in mine for sure - as we moved along the stony track under the aurora of background noise. I was due to leave the group a little further along the path but we never got there. We suddenly came under intense machine gun fire (a peculiar type of sound once heard never forgotten) and we immediately threw ourselves down in all directions. I rolled into a shallow depression and stayed there. It was bitterly cold but I was bathed in the sweat of fear with an overall feeling of utter helplessness. The bullets pinged and sung around the place. It was obvious that several of the Yanks had been hit judging by the shouts and screams but how seriously I never learned.

During the long dark hours that followed, the area was sprayed by spasmodic machine gun fire. Occasionally the area was illuminated by star shells, and if I could have got deeper into my depression, I would have done so. Flashes, fireflies of tracer here and there flying between the small hills, and the general noise bouncing back and forth. My soldier friends had faded away somewhere; I felt very much alone. Worst of all, I was completely and utterly disorientated. I stayed in my depression all through that long night without the slightest idea of where I was. Through the following day, I slowly and carefully took stock of my position. I was very thirsty and hungry too, and I ached in every joint. I began to doubt if I would ever be able to crawl out when the time came but while it was light, I was definitely unwilling to try. All through that long, long day the area was swept by that machine gun at irregular intervals. I was sure 'they' could see me but towards the end of the day I got the impression that it was sighted blind, never-the-less I could not bring myself to move.

The stony ground was very anti-infantry compared with the soft sand of my, now, beloved desert. Even the stony ground of the desert was friendlier than that of Cassino from the point of view of ricochets and the facility of being able to scrape a quick fox-hole.

When darkness eventually fell, I made the supreme effort to shift myself and got out moving in the direction I had finally decided I had to go. By-the-time I reached the forward unit to which I had had originally been ordered to, the information I carried was out-of-date. The guys shared their rations with me before directing me back by a somewhat safer route than the one I had come up on. Things were constantly changing within the relatively small forward distances of the Cassino (Gustav) Line at that time.

The three main avenues of communication were the radio, overland telephone lines and the physical act of carrying messages  by D.R.'s and 'Ground Runners'. Each had their Pro's and Con's of course. In the semi-static situation applying in front of Cassino, phone lines literally lying on the ground were often fractured by shells and shrapnel etc.,

The casualties amongst D.R.'s was frighteningly high. Within a couple of weeks of our arrival, two of the lads of the four of us who left Foggia together had been killed on this Cassino front and the third of my quartet was very badly injured within a month. I was told later that he had lost a leg, but I never actually saw him again.

The days and nights passed, then one bright morning I found myself at a point somewhere east of Cassino, from where I could just see the monastery on the hill. Everyone hated the place, we knew for sure that 'Jerry' up there could see everything, all we were doing; in fact, our every move. Day in, day out, he was watching us from up there. The noise, the continuous reverberations of the incessant cracks and whoomps bouncing back and forth from the hills, in front of you, behind you, on top of you. The ever present stomach turning fear and even when you thought you were over the worst, you realised that you still had the feeling of hard walnuts in your chest. For those who have experienced what I am trying to describe, will know how inadequate my description is.

One hardly ever saw the enemy, except dead, other than a fleeting glimpse. A glimpse so fleeting that you almost doubted if you had actually seen someone. You hoped that you were as successful at hiding and keeping low. You had to be or you would be dead. Then you had the uncomfortable knowledge, at the back of your mind, that up there in the accursed monastery, they could see your every move. Strange, but we know that any high point gives advantage to the occupier but it was the monastery, Monte Cassino, that we hated so. It was the monastery we blamed for all our discomforts and ills.

Then they came; our bombers!

We watched in silent amazement as Monte Cassino disappeared under a cloud of dust and exploding bombs. Then we started to cheer, with all our voice and hearts, we started to cheer. God, how we cheered! Then I got careless and started to jump up but I was quickly floored by a kick in the back of my knees. In the excitement of the moment, I had stupidly risked all. No-one would admit to pulling me down but I may well owe my life to that friend.

February into March and slowly the

Army moved up Via Route Six, nearer into the town of Cassino which had already been under heavy shell fire for some time. Route Six headed directly towards Monte Cassino through the original town of Cassino (the modern town is a mile west of the old one), before turning left through 90 degrees and then turning right for Rome around the Massive. Although the Germans were still up among the ruins of the Abbey, we didn't seem to mind quite as much.

Then our bombers came over in strength again and pounded the town of Cassino so utterly that it was difficult to find one stone standing on another. But once again, the debris made an advance by tanks impossible and the debris provided good cover for the German defenders. I guess I was about ten miles away when the first of the real bombing attacks were made but even so, the extra noise was terrific and the huge cloud of dust that was Cassino climbed for 'miles' into the air. Some of the bombs however fell wide and a number of our own units were hit including a Signals Centre, which I often had to use. I lost half-a-dozen mates there in one go.

Further south, nature was showing off her own abilities of pyrotechnic displays because Vesuvius was erupting furiously and in spite of all that was going on, it was a major topic of our 'chit chat'; a kind of release from the 'normal' day-to-day happenings.

Although it is now customary to refer to the Battle of Cassino, there were, in fact, four battles. All were hard slogging infantry battles reminiscent of World War I, and I know now that the casualty figures were as high as any from 1914 - 1918.

The 'Castle' ruins are on the hill in the centre of the picture below Monte Cassino Abbey.

Over the next few months I was going to and from around the Cassino mountain, over the Rapido River, back in and near to parts of Cassino town. The nearest I got to Monte Cassino during the actual war operations was Castle Hill. The Castle was built on a steep rocky knoll, about 300 feet high, and is linked by a saddle of rock to the Monastery Hill. About 400 or 500 yards away and some 700 feet below the monastery wall there was a small pinnacle of rock on which stood a broken pylon that once had carried some kind of rope causeway from the town to the monastery. From some angles, it looked like giblet so it acquired the name of Hangman's Hill. Several times I had had to make my way up Castle Hill, I would have said 'in the dark', but the shells and mortars crashing among the rocks would burst in flashes of flame and red light causing flints to fly along with the deadly shards of steel. Occasionally, when the main barrage seemed to quieten, one would hear the rip of German Spandau answered by the slower rattle of a British Bren gun. Worst of all, for someone like me, was the ever present threat of the sniper although, of course, I would have never have heard the one that counted.

I once had to get to a platoon on the west slope only to find that they had all been killed by mortar fire. I stayed there for some time to collect myself before stumbling back down the escarpment to a sangar. (A sangar is a hollow with a stone breastwork) The fact that I had got in and out indicated the enemy were in no better state than we were. Several of my old associates from that time lie forever in the Cassino Railway Station graveyard

Then suddenly it was all over. At least for me, Cassino was over.

I got detailed back to Naples and was surprised and happy to find that I was destined to go to a temporary R & R camp. (Rest and Recuperation) I walked into the Signals Orderly Room in Naples and was given a special pass. Before I realised it I was shipped over to the Isle of Capri, a rest home mainly for commissioned men. Good food, clean sheets, warm water and swimming, even a visit to the Blue Grotto. Marvellous! Athough it was wonderful, I have often wondered why I was selected. I can only assume that the records (notoriously bad at that time) were some-what confusing. Since officers carry revolvers, and as a D.R. I carried one, my dishevelled condition and DR boots did not deter the orderlies from thinking that I was an officer! Anyway, I was there for eleven or ten blistering days before I was embarrassingly sent to the Provost Marshal's Office for my new movement orders. In the event, I collected a new bike from the Naples Dock Stores then proceeded back to my old squadron in Foggia, to John, to my old desert bed and to my little dog Bobbie.

It was to be many years before I began to regret the destruction of the Abbey but how can you really select that one event in isolation from the rest of the carnage.

Memories not recorded here used to haunt me, but Monte Cassino is now at peace.

CHAPTER TWELVE

FORWARD TO ROME

BACK ON THE SQUADRON AT Foggia, I was "put out" to find that John had been promoted to a Sergeant (of Motor Transport Fitters) and had been posted to the Wing Head Quarters. In actual fact, he had moved about a mile away around the airfield perimeter. It did mean that he fed and drank in the Sergeant's Mess, whereas I was still an L.A.C. (Leading Aircraftsman) which is equivalent to a Lance Corporal. In practice, I found that I was the most invited L.A.C. to frequent the Sergeants Mess at the Wing.

Foggia Main was by now a really vast airfield complex, being home to American Flying Fortress Wings and American Thunderbolt and Lightning fighter squadrons, as well as our own British Wellington Group of bombers consisting of about eight squadrons.

The bombing war had been going on steadily while I had been away. I was astounded to learn the extent of our bomber losses, mainly in attacks in the Balkans, some mine dropping operations in the Danube and a number of important attacks in Northern Italy. I was also surprised to hear that a Lightning had one day come screaming down from heights unmentionable, without the pilot, and had had the audacity to hurl itself at the Intelligence tent. To my chagrin, it missed, but I heard that the Intelligence Officer, who was in the latrine at the time, had to go back to it in a hurry when he realised how close the plane came to ending his young life. Not so funny was the fact that one of the long range petrol tanks had followed the plane down and apparently bounced over my empty tent into the vineyard beyond. The poor American pilot had supposedly hit the tail unit as he had baled out. From a great height, he had hung limply in his parachute and died of injuries and frostbite on the way down.

In the early days of June 1944, with Cassino out of the way, Rome actually fell. A day or two afterward we heard that there had been the long awaited invasion of Europe in Normandy.

In the coming months, I spent my time travelling between my Squadron Intelligence Officers, my Wing and Group executives, and across to Naples. Then I started running up to Rome as well.

As I have already said, John had been promoted to a Sergeant, was at Wing HQ, and had taken the dogs with him. My little tent, including my odds and ends, was left by the vineyard but John had my bed with him. John's tent was about a mile or so from mine. As the days went by, Bobbie and I would spend our leisure hours with John, Barbara, and Bobbie's brother, which John had named Killer. Killer, was as soft as they come, the little cad pup who no one else wanted.

Bobbie was a wonderfully clever little mongrel. When I was going off on a job I'd say something like "Go see John" and once Bobbie saw me waving to him as I moved out down the track on my bike, he would trot over to John at the Wing. John told me that the dog would leave him every now and again to check my tent to see if I'd come back. Anyway, it was a fact that I could be certain that within a couple of hours or so of my return, he'd be bounding in, a little energetic bundle of tail wagging brown dog with a tongue nearly as long as his tail.

I used to take him to the mess tent for tea, and after I had had mine, I would let him lap-up some from my mug. He loved it. The carpenter, who was a kindly soul, thought it would be nicer if the dog had his own mug. (It's hard to credit this when one really appreciates how we were living at the time.) One day, he took the trouble to carve him one out from a block of wood, complete with a handle. It became a joke to see me and my dog going down together for our tea. To complete the joke, I taught Bobbie to carry his own mug. But the real joke was on me because one day when I was away, Bobbie took his own mug to the mess and the cook filled him up and slated me to pay for it when I got back!

Bobbie used to sleep on my bed with me and would go for anyone who had the temerity to try to wake me up; and that would include the Duty Officer when I was on standby. All kinds of diversions were adopted to attract my attention when I was asleep, without incurring Bobbie's wroth!

My tent was pitched in the vineyard on the edge of the south runway of Foggia, a most delightful spot. When the grapes came into season Bobbie learnt to chew them on the vine and all the grapes within his reach for hundreds of yards around were mere skins on bare stalks. He would stand there with the grapes hanging in his mouth, chewing with his lips curled back with the juice literally running out of his jowl.

Once, when I was going to Naples for a weekend, I left the camp on the back of a

lorry with about a dozen other chaps. Bobbie knew this was different to the bike and would not be left behind and, consequently, ran after the lorry for several miles. I implored and threatened from the lorry as we bounced along and all the chaps in the lorry with me shouted and hooted but still the little tyke ran after us; it was almost as though he thought we were encouraging him to run faster! It began to wear thin because it became obvious that I was going to make the lorry go back with my dog and me. When eventually the lorry stopped, only Bobbie and I were pleased. I then got the driver to take Bobbie and me back to camp. I was not popular with the lads but I didn't care. What could be better than spending the whole of my "free" weekend with Bobbie doing what he liked best, chasing lizards through the grape vines! Ah well!!

But I must go back to the early days of

June/July '44 before I race on. I started to make a regular run over the lower Apennines to Naples from Foggia via Benevento. The town of Benevento was once famous for a kind of liqueur and nougat but in mid '44 it became notorious as being the centre of black market activities. The value of the grain of Foggia appreciated out of all proportion once it was transported to Naples, so the road out of Foggia was crowded with young girls with sacks of corn begging lifts from service lorry drivers.

Payment was negotiable!

I'd only been settled in my tent for a couple of days when in the early hours of one morning, a Wellington came in and on touch down blew up with the usual tremendous crack and leaping fire, followed by the crackling noises of small arms ammunition going off. A hung up bomb fell off on landing and exploded beneath the aircraft blowing off the tail and part of the midship. The pilot and bomb aimer survived, the remainder of the crew died however. I often questioned why a jettisonable bomb rack had never been designed to get over this "bombs hung up" problem.

I wondered about the position of my tent on the edge of the south runway but decided that, all considered, it was a desirable site.

Then in early July, we had another tragedy concerning a Wellington but this time on take-off. A huge flash at the end of the runway was the first indication that all was not well. Sparks had been seen coming from one engine. Unfortunately for all concerned, the Wellington ploughed in with a 4000-pound blockbuster bomb, which exploded on contact.

All this was happening day by day, in addition to the losses from raids at night by the British airmen and the huge losses suffered by the Americans with their daylight offensive. There was always something going adrift and a resounding crunch from the other side of Foggia Main followed by a tall column of dirty brown smoke invariably meant that something had happened to a Fortress and its dangerous load.

We also had a couple of cases of Wellingtons stalling. New crews always had to have practice "circuits and bumps," and that's exactly what it was. They had to fly around the airfield coming in as though to land, touch their wheels on the ground then put full power on to go around again. One of the accidents was caused by the pilot flying very low and pulling up quickly to 1000 feet when an engine cut out. The aircraft stalled and fell like a stone. All four men flying at the time were killed and the Wimpy was utterly destroyed The other was caused by a late decision to go round again after nearly touching down with the propellers having been left in coarse pitch. The result was a very heavy flop from about ten feet just over the airfield perimeter. No one was injured but there was a badly damaged aeroplane and some very dented pride.

By arrangement with my Intelligence Officer, I went off to Naples knowing that I would be going on to Rome. From Naples, I opted to go up to Rome on Route Six; I just had to go up through Cassino. As I rode through the utter devastation of the town of Cassino close under Castle Hill and the still overpowering pile of debris on Monastery Hill; my hackles were prickling. I had expected the worst. Soldiers and civilians, in small groups, were moving over the town ruins. I knew that the soldiers and civilians were looking for different things. It had been six weeks or so since the line moved forward, but there were still some last duties to perform. The official casualty figure recorded for The Battles of Cassino was 50,000. An unbelievable 4,000 were listed simply as missing.

As I entered Rome, I was immediately struck by the general well-being of the population. They looked clean and well fed compared with the generally unwashed, unkempt scallywags of Naples. The buildings too, they were different, all the ruins were two thousand years old!

I visited St Peters and wandered around that vast church in splendid isolation, my D.R. boots echoing on the marble floor. I was approached by some kind of church official who tried to tell me that I couldn't use a camera (millions of visitors take billions of pictures now-a-days), but I was in no mood to take orders from an Italian, even if he was a churchman. (Endemic of the times I suppose) I ambled about and after some time I found my way into the inner sanctum of the Vatican City and I finally walked slowly through the amazingly beautiful Sistine Chapel. At the time I had no idea how privileged I was. Ultimately I was gently shown the way out by a concerned church officer.

I rode across Rome to the Coliseum. I recall it was a little chilly and it had rained a bit. In those days, there were no railings around the structure and one could gain access exactly in the same way as the ancient Romans had done. There were no iron gates and no "way in" signs leading to the ticket boxes as now! Once again, I wandered in and around the building on my lonesome. It was a little eerie in the falling light as the cool evening breeze whipped dust up and down the darkening stone corridors. I was very impressed. In one's imagination, you could go back fifteen hundred years very easily, unlike today, crowded with the peoples of all nations and their clicking cameras. In that vast skeleton of an arena with its tiers of stone terraces, ones mind drew pictures of the ancient man-made cruelty that transpired at this spot. My thoughts at that time and only six weeks after Cassino!

Leaving the Coliseum I passed the Roman Forum without realising what it was. I am shamefaced to say that I had no idea what the Forum ruins were and gave the huge mass of marble that is the monument of Vittorio Emanuele just a cursory glance on my way out of Rome. The Emanuele monument became a landmark and was known to all and sundry as "The Wedding Cake."

Back at Foggia Main, the British camp facilities were very basic indeed, even though we made a great many local "improvements." Some of us were surprised, to say the very least, to discover that our American friends had imported some large ice cream and ice cube making equipment. What some might consider as frivolous was, in fact, essential material for the welfare of the Americans—a wonderful moral booster for them, with a spin-off for some of us British. We got into an internal trading market, not black just a little grey, a kind of swapping business. A bottle of whisky (from the Sergeant's mess) was worth half a dozen cases of Carnation Evaporated Milk - a great favourite of Bobbie's! My American friends would never haggle; they would gladly swap six or more tins of Spam for one of our Corned Beef. Strangely enough though, you could eat Corned Beef for so much longer than Spam without tiring of it. Spam was so highly seasoned for our taste, never-the-less, a wonderful change.

One of the times that John and I got together with some Yanks in their tent, we sat around telling stories of training, amusing war tales and the like while we drank their coffee. Someone made a remark about how good it would be to have an instantly made coffee. I don't know if they had an "instant" in those days or not, but we told them of our desert "instant tea." Desert "Tea Mix" was a dry powder concoction of tea, milk and sugar supplied in airtight tins. It was a God-sent brew for us in the desert, and passed as our "char." (Tea)

An Aside

After the war, following a two year photographic and cinematography course at the Regent Street Polytechnic in London and a year freelancing in Fleet Street, I was being interviewed by a Director of United Dairies for a full-time regular photographic job. In answer to questions about my wartime service, I gratuitously remarked on certain conditions in the Western Desert, and what a lifesaver a thing called Tea Mix was. It transpired that the man interviewing me was Professor Edward Capstick, one time holder of the Chair of Dairying at the Reading University, who had conceived and pioneered Tea Mix.

I got the job and stayed with the company for more than 39 years.

Through the warm days of July and August of 44, our Group of bombers attacked oil refineries at Trieste and a couple of places called Bosanski and Almasfrizito, as well as hitting numerous railway junctions and doing some mine laying in the Danube. I rode to and from, up and down, the dusty tracks and roads full of military traffic, delivering my despatches. John and I regularly visited our American chums and did swaps on bigger and bigger scales. The only shady deal I ever got involved in with them, was to act as a British D.R. escorting half a tanker load of American aviation fuel, thereby giving the journey credibility, which we delivered to the back streets of Benevento. I didn't mind too much because there was a lot of cash around and the high-octane petrol was so unsuitable for their cars that it was bound to damage them.

There was so much skulduggery going on that it was difficult to keep up with it all. One day there was a great hue and cry around the camp. It transpired that some Italians had taken a couple of blankets, which had been left out to "sun" to discourage fleas and lice. We all went chasing out to catch the thieves. In my search on the airfield perimeter, I went past a farmhouse from which a huge dog came flashing out barking and viciously trying to bite my leg. I slipped my clutch and cowboy-like whipped out my revolver and banged a shot at it. It yelped and ran back to the farmhouse. After collecting myself, I returned to the farmhouse as well, revolver in hand. By-the-time I got there, the whole family, including two or three men, had the dog on the bare kitchen table. Amid a babble of voices and the growls of the dog, they were showing me that the bullet was lodged in the loose fur in the top of the dog's neck. They were all very angry, and one man came round the table in a threatening manner but stopped short, probably because of my revolver, which had pointedly followed him round. I would have put a bullet into him rather than the dog if the truth were known and I think the message got through to him. I retreated with as much dignity as I could muster.

Group records show that during September 44, we had two Wellingtons collide over the Ferrara rail yard target but incredibly both aircraft returned safely to Foggia. Later in the same month, a Wellington came back from bombing Brescia West rail yard with its tail damaged and its rear turret missing including the poor gunner. By the nature of the damage, it was assumed that it was cut off by a bomb from another Wellington. I distinctly remember the turret incident because it so intrigued our American friends that they came over in droves to view the aeroplane.

October and the rains came; my God, how the rains came! Tents were flooded like everything else. Beds, equipment, clothes, everything sodden. All operations were cancelled because our Wellingtons couldn't take off from the flooded field. Somehow the Americans got back to work a couple of days before we did, although I don't know how.

In the meantime, we had a Mosquito crash-land very badly on our ground and bits of aeroplane were everywhere. One of our chaps surreptitiously helped himself to pieces of radio equipment which he thought would come in useful in the new craze of making ones own radio set. We all had radios of one kind or another, and our sneak-thief was into building sets, at a price, for the lads. What he didn't know was that a great deal of the equipment was so very secret that it had a built-in destruction device but it hadn't triggered off correctly. He badly damaged his hands when he put some voltage across some questionable component. He had to face service discipline, which was pretty tough on him. The Americans ran a local radio station from Foggia with programs of news, chitchat, and music. The Foggia broadcaster always use to start his morning transmission with: "This is the old speckled boid (bird) on his nest in Foggia saying, 'Wherever you are, wherever you be, lots and lots of good luck to you on your job today and above all, take care of thee.'"

The Abruzzi Missif, highest of the Appenine range, is in a harsh region and is somewhat isolated. The road to Rome across the country was well defined but the surface and size of carriageway varied considerably. The area is wooded with oak and beech on the lower slopes followed, higher up, by conifers; above that comes the mountain pastures swept, at times, by high winds. I learnt that there were several plateaux but it was, generally, very dangerous country. It was not terrain suitable for modern mechanised warfare but German and British troops had each passed through it. I had reason to travel across the area once on the lower pass to Rome but the weather deteriorated rapidly and I was glad to get to a village where, luckily, I was accepted as a friend. I was fed by a family who obviously had some standing in the community. I was introduced to several Italians, one of whom was the mayor. The "mayor," however, was bogus; he just didn't fit in properly. When I left, he smiled at me slyly. He was a deserter, of that, I am absolutely sure!

As the year of 1944 came to it's close, we honestly couldn't see the end of the Italian campaign. Our troops and Allies had been stuck against the German Gothic Line for quite some time and, although there were a number of local successes, there was no real sign that a complete breakout was imminent. But one had to cheer up because a great deal seemed to be happening in the rest of Europe.

Christmas 1944, my fourth one away from England and home.

CHAPTER THIRTEEN

CHIANTI COUNTRY

THE NEW YEAR OPENED WITH all kinds of rumours doing the rounds. The main one was that the squadron was going to move on again but it was difficult to see where it could sensibly go. Some wishful thinking prompted England as a destination but the consensus of considered opinion was that it was "not bloody likely!"

However, not on the rumour list but the first important change was that we were to loose our faithful Wellington bombers for the much larger four engine Liberators. Conversion to the new bombers began in early January and continued through February to become the operational aircraft of the squadron by March. The second important thing was that I was not to see the conversion program finished because I got a permanent posting. I had to leave my dog Bobbie, John and all the familiar things of Foggia and go my relatively lonely way north to Arezzo. It was a great wrench. I'd been with John since those very early days of 1942 in Kabrit. We had the inevitable binge and drank ourselves silly (as though that would help). John said he'd look after Bobbie, made arrangements to have my little one man tent moved and I gave him "the bed." We agreed to keep in touch, and away I went, waving Bobbie "Goodbye"!

Along to Benevento, up across to Cassino and on to Rome, then north into Tuscany to Arezzo in the heart of the Chianti country. I joined a Repair and Salvage Unit based near the small hill town of Arezzo, some sixty or seventy miles south of Florence.

The R & S Unit comprised of half a dozen of the new huge Tank Transporters, numerous drivers, and fitters and a few motorcyclists (D.R.'s). The motorcyclists acted as scouts to follow up on reports of disabled tanks and other vehicles to ascertain the possibility of recovery. We all had a rapid course on the problems involved in tank recovery. Somehow, it was never mentioned that the enemy wasn't too keen on our activity and often had left a small, but effective, reception committee.

It was still a slogging match up front, breaking through the Gothic Line was still not easy. A great deal of the shifting of men and material from one sector to another seemed to be going on. I was kept so busy going out of Arezzo to the satellite depots, which were situated near the front, that I hardly had time to think or worry. The very heavy large transporters that I had to guide and generally look after were a challenge, no less for the drivers and fitters themselves. All kinds of damaged battlewagons were collected from all kinds of unimaginable places, at times, under the noses of the enemy. I admired those drivers so much. Often the German snipers let the D.R. come and go so as to reap the bigger reward of transport drivers and fitters!

The local industry seemed to be wine making so I was quickly introduced to the very many variants of their staple product.

April saw a great deal of movement in my sector as things fell apart for the German army. A highly confused and dangerous situation was developing where some enemy units were surrendering while other units fought like cornered tigers. It wasn't safe to take anything or anyone for granted. It never had been, of course, but now one was lulled into a sense of false security because of some units giving up.

Then the war was officially over in Italy, followed by the end in Europe.

For the next two months, I continued to work steadily with the Repair and Salvage Unit but now it was without any anxiety. I began to appreciate the beautiful countryside and, for awhile, acquired a taste for the many kinds of

Chianti.

The whole R & S Unit moved up to a camp near Bologna. From the surrounding area a great deal of war material was collected but I had barely been up there for a month or so when it was announced that the Far East War had ended following the dropping of a "special" bomb!

At about the same time I received my repatriation notice and had to go all the way back down to Naples. I could never understand that. Anyway, on the way down I had another look at Cassino.

I never got back to Foggia, to see John and his dogs, or my good little friend Bobbie - probably as well! John had the unenviable task of shooting the dogs (including my Bobbie). We couldn't bring them back to England and no one wanted to just leave them in Italy.

At the Transit Camp in Naples I turned in my bike but kept my revolver and started the long, long wait for transport back to England.

Chapter Fourteen

BACK to ENGLAND

AT LONG LAST I WAS off. I had to suffer the indignity (for a D.R.) of travelling in the back of a succession of lorries for three or four days it took us to get up to Milan. It was a journey that seemed never to end. Then into another Transit Camp before being herded, with hundreds of others, to Milan railway station. The journey across Europe seemed interminable. Whenever the train stopped, and it was often, armed guards got out and stood along the carriages. I never knew whether it was to stop us getting off - perish the thought - or to stop strangers getting on.

Going north the train eventually went through a very long Swiss tunnel finally breaking out into the French countryside. After more than a week, we were unloaded somewhere near Calais. Another day in a Transit Camp where we were equipped with some warmer clothes. It was here that I had to hand in my revolver, with the original six rounds of ammunition that I had always carried wrapped in a small piece of oiled lint.

Finally, we embarked to cross the English Channel and were nearly brought to tears at the sight of the White Cliffs of Dover. On landing, we travelled by train and road to Hornchurch in Essex.

I was there for about a week being fully re-equipped with everything an airman needs, or doesn't need, complete with an overcoat that I did need! After so long away it seemed strange to hear everyone speaking English and the fact that one could drink water straight from the tap impressed me no end; and the money, it was pounds, shillings and pence!

At last, I was on my way home to Harwich.

I caught the train from Liverpool Street station in London. I had to change and wait at Manningtree station for about an hour, with half-a-dozen other people, for the local connecting train for Dovercourt and Harwich. Harwich is the end of the line and the platform reflects that. All the passengers got off at Dovercourt - except me. Eventually the train puffed the last mile into the deserted Harwich line-end, and as I got off, I could see the tall, slim figure of my mother standing beside my father at the open platform's end. I swung my new kitbag over my shoulder as we all started to walk towards each other. When we were about ten yards apart I stopped, dropped my kitbag and, as my father was in his Royal Marine uniform (he was a Lt. Colonel) I gave him the best salute I could muster! My mother just threw her arms around me (the first and only time she ever did anything like that). My father just held out his hand for a handshake, which I recall I grasped. Once that moment was over my father swung my kitbag over his shoulder (afterwards I thought how I would have loved my old mates to have seen that!) while my mother held my arm talking two hundred to a dozen. We all walked slowly back to the house on Albert Street, the one on the Bathside of Harwich - the house to which she had gone to, alone, way back in November 1940.

It was now September 1945 and we were all home.

EPILOGUE

THE WAR WAS OVER, YET I still had another year in the service before I was demobbed.

While I was heading back to England, John and the squadrons were heading towards Abu Suier in Egypt. By the time they had all arrived there, John was due for repatriation and was immediately turned round back to England. He was lucky, in a way, because he came back via Transport Air Command so it didn't take him quite as long. I was eventually to learn that he, and one of the drivers from the motor transport section, had shot all the dogs before leaving Italy and that included my Bobbie. It was the best for them, but I am glad that I wasn't there to have to do it!

During my leave, I went up to Shirley near Birmingham to see Berenice. It was to be the first time since 1941. I travelled to Birmingham's Snow Street station but she wasn't there to meet me. (In actual fact she was there but we missed each other) I found my way to the Bull Ring bus station and got on the bus for Shirley. Unbeknown to me Berenice was inside the bus as I went upstairs. She thought she recognised me, but wasn't sure. (Well, it had been nearly five years) I got off the bus several stops before I should have and I was astounded to hear a voice say "Why did you get off here?" As we walked together from the bus stop home, our conversation was punctuated with long pauses. I eventually took Berenice to Harwich to meet my mother and father.

After my leave, I had to report to Rivenhall in Essex. I did practically nothing while I was there, but I was luckily introduced to the RAF Further Education Scheme.

I realised that it would not be too long before I would be out of the service and looking for a job, but what job? I would be 24 years of age. The Educational Officer wheedled out of me that I was keen on photography and I romantically fancied a job in the motion picture world, the film industry. In January 1946, I discovered that there was a two-year, full time Photographic and Cinematography course at the Polytechnic, Regent Street, London. I also found that they required matriculation standard of education as a basic condition of entry. As I was deficient of any certificate, I would have to take an entrance examination.

In February 1946, I was posted to No. 4 Group Headquarters in York, as a D.R. of course. There was a regular weekly run from Group HQ to the RAF Records situated in the Great Park of Hampton Court. None of the D.R.'s based in York wanted the job - they thought it too far! What a dream! Once a week down to Hampton Court with a detour to Birmingham, and Berenice on the way back. The rest of the week I studied the contents of the syllabus arranged for me by the really helpful Educational Officer in York. He had received a note, concerning me from his colleague in Rivenhall; a helping hand is all you need. They really did do their job and I have to say that I always appreciated their concern for an ordinary airman.

My father was one of the first to be demobbed and he and my mother had come back to London. They had acquired a council controlled flat in a large house in the Old Kent Road. My father was offered a "Grace and Favour" apartment in St James' Palace but mother was frightened of pomp and ceremony and refused to go to it.

John came back safely from Egypt and was demobbed and took up again with his pre-war girl friend Doreen. He was demobbed just before I was and here is a street picture of a civilian father and a civilian John on either side of a scruffy airman, strolling down Oxford Street. I was sent to the demob centre in June 1946 and collected my grey chalk striped suit and my papers that said I was now released.

Berenice and I went to John's wedding in Rochester in Kent and I was his best man. John and Doreen came to the wedding of Berenice and me in Shirley and John was my best man.

Berenice and I went to live with my mother and father in the Old Kent Road. I successfully passed my entrance exam for the Polytechnic and started my two year Cinematography course in September 1946. I went on a grant of £2 and an extra 10 shillings a week as a married man.

I was officially discharged from the service in October 1946. In a totally unexplained frenzy, I immediately got rid of my uniform and burnt my paybook, an action I later regretted.

This is the end of this, but the start of all that followed!

Editor's Note: Eric Merry also completed a continuance of his story after the war: The Penguin's New Suit.

ABOUT THE AUTHOR

Eric Merry is an English World War II veteran who served in the Royal Air Force from 1940-1946, one year in England as an air gunner and the rest in North Africa and Italy as a dispatch rider. When he returned home, he found a devastated, war-torn England. Through hard work and perseverance, he became an industrial photographer and then a public affairs director for the largest retail milk company in the world. After retiring, he wrote Penguin's Progress, a memoir of his war experiences, for his son and grandson. The book has since been accepted as an archival research document by the Imperial War Museum in London. Merry currently lives in the United States near Chicago, but has visited England often.